Days
Demanding
Courage

Days
Demanding
Courage

by Harold Blake Walker

Rand McNally & Company
Chicago • New York • San Francisco

Acknowledgments

Quotations reprinted courtesy of the following publishers:
"Beyond the Storm," by Grantland Rice, from *Only the Brave,* Copyright 1941. Reprinted by permission of A. S. Barnes & Co., Inc.
"Western Star," by Stephen Vincent Benét, Copyright 1943. Reprinted by permission of Brandt & Brandt.
"Washington at Valley Forge," by Viney Wilder Endicott, Copyright 1967. Reprinted by permission of the author.
"Prayer," by Louis Untermeyer, Copyright 1914, by Harcourt Brace Jovanovich, Inc.; renewed 1942, by Louis Untermeyer. From *Long Feud* by Louis Untermeyer. "Burnt Norton," by T. S. Eliot, in *Four Quartets,* Copyright 1943, by T. S. Eliot; renewed 1971, by Esme Valerie Eliot. *Murder in the Cathedral,* by T. S. Eliot, Copyright 1952, by Harcourt Brace Jovanovich, Inc. *The Cocktail Party,* by T. S. Eliot, Copyright 1950, by Harcourt Brace Jovanovich, Inc. All reprinted by permission of Harcourt Brace Jovanovich, Inc.
"Beclouded," by Emily Dickinson, from *The Poems of Emily Dickinson,* edited by Thomas H. Johnson, Cambridge, Mass. The Belknap Press of Harvard University Press. Copyright 1951, 1955 by the President and Fellows of Harvard College. Reprinted by permission of the publishers and the Trustees of Amherst College.
"The Census Taker" and "There Are Roughly Zones," by Robert Frost, from *The Complete Poems of Robert Frost,* Copyright 1949, by Holt, Rinehart & Winston. Reprinted by permission of Holt, Rinehart & Winston.
"King Jasper," by Edwin Arlington Robinson, Copyright 1935, by Macmillan Publishing Co., Inc.; renewed 1963, by Macmillan Publishing Co., Inc. "Captain Craig," by Edwin Arlington Robinson, Copyright 1915, by Edwin Arlington Robinson; renewed 1943, by Ruth Nivison. Both from *Collected Poems of Edwin Arlington Robinson.* Reprinted by permission of Macmillan Publishing Co., Inc.
The Firstborn, by Christopher Fry, Copyright 1952, by Oxford University Press. Reprinted by permission of Oxford University Press.
"Winter," by Walter de la Mare, from *Collected Poems of Walter de la Mare,* Copyright 1941. Reprinted by permission of The Literary Trustees of Walter de la Mare and the Society of Authors as their representative.
Epic of America, by James Truslow Adams, Little Brown and Co., 1931, by permission.
Long Day's Journey into Night, by Eugene O'Neill, Yale University Press, 1956, by permission.

All the essays in this book previously appeared in the *Chicago Tribune Magazine.*

Library of Congress Cataloging in Publication Data

Walker, Harold Blake.
    Days demanding courage.
    Selections from a column that the author has written
for many years for the Chicago Tribune Magazine.
    1. Christian life—Addresses, essays, lectures.
I. Title
BV4501.2.W314   248'.4   78-7099
ISBN 0-528-81864-3

First printing, 1978

Contents

Wisdom for Our Time

Foundations for Tomorrow

Introduction

A wild wind is blowing through the cultural landscape of the nation, uprooting many of the hallowed traditions of our yesterdays and sweeping away the spiritual topsoil that has nourished our ethical standards in the past. The untamed wind has eroded our faith in government, in business, and in the institutions that have been sources of personal and national strength and stability.

Untroubled in our affluence, we did not notice the ravages of the wild wind. With plenty of everything, ideals and values seemed unimportant. We neglected the things of the spirit, leaning our lives on material props. Permissiveness reigned supreme in our goalless culture and left us devoid of meaning and purpose. So it was that the fibers of the American dream unraveled in our hands.

Now, under the stress of our personal and national problems, ranging from emotional illnesses to inflation and from family disintegration to the energy shortage, we may be coming to our senses and discovering that these are days demanding courage if we are to tame the wild wind. There are signs that the American dream is coming alive again, along with old-fashioned faith and confidence that we can cope with our ills and create a better land for ourselves and our children.

We are taking a fresh look at the faith of our fathers and finding it living still in our minds and hearts. The amazing growth of the evangelical movement has made us aware of the yearning of the many for a strong defense against the erosion of the wild wind. If we are not "born again," at least we are rediscovering the significance of the moral values of our Puritan inheritance and demanding decency in politics, business, and personal life.

We still love our "land of the free and the home of the brave," with her glorious mountains, plains, and "the cattle on a thousand hills." We are grateful for memories of pioneers and patriots whose courage has enriched our heritage. Our spines tingle when we sing "God Bless America," and our emotions are stirred by "The Star Spangled Banner." Our cynicism is only skin deep, and, despite our attempts to be blasé, we cherish this "land of the noble free."

The wild wind has left enough of our spiritual topsoil to nourish renewed faith in ourselves, our nation, and its sustaining institutions. It may be that the ills of which we are aware have made us conscious of our need for courage to undergird our integrity and for faith to buttress our loyalty to the noblest values we know. Our troubles can be the source of our redemption. Adversity has its compensations and hardship often yields hardihood. Discouragement and difficulty make us aware of our need for God, for wisdom, and courage beyond our own.

Girded with the wisdom of God, we may yet tame the wild wind and use it to fashion our souls, revive the American dream, and guide the land we love with intelligent faith. The hope of the nation is in the spirit of the people who share it, in our will to shape it into "some diviner mold," and our resolution to be both worthy and responsible citizens.

Throughout the past twenty-seven years, I have been writing a column about people, their problems, their hopes and their hurts, and their part in shaping the land we love. The column has been published in the *Chicago Tribune Magazine* and, for many years, was syndicated by the Chicago Tribune-New York News Syndicate. The present volume represents a selection of the best pieces from the column and is offered in the hope that it may be helpful in restoring the faith and confidence of readers in themselves and in their nation.

I am indebted to my wife, Mary Alice, for her invaluable assistance in selecting the essays for this volume, to Mrs. James Page for her careful preparation of the manuscript, and to the editors of Rand McNally & Company, for their gracious encouragement.

Harold Blake Walker

Evanston, Illinois

This Is My Land

We have a long and arduous road to travel if we are to realize our American dream in the life of our nation, but if we fail, there is nothing left but the old eternal round. The alternative is the failure of self government, the failure of the common man to rise to full stature, the failure of all that the American dream has held of hope and promise for mankind.

"Our American Dream"
by JAMES TRUSLOW ADAMS

Land That I Love

The land that I love is filled with contradictions, ambiguities, and paradoxes. It is the grandeur of towering skyscrapers and the sinister danger of dark alleys, the comfort and affluence of high-rise apartments and the misery of the ghettos, the wealth of the suburbs and the decay of the cities, the splendor of museums and art galleries and the graffiti on subway walls.

It would be easy to paint a grim portrait of my land, with its air, lakes, rivers, and brooks polluted; its hills and valleys littered by the careless; its streets unsafe after dark; its conflicts tearing the social fabric; its political and business corruption threatening our free-enterprise system. The ills of my land are all too obvious.

Happily, however, the negatives pale beside the positives in this "land of the free and home of the brave." James Dickey commented recently that Woody Guthrie said somewhere, or should have said: "The true sound of the American people is the sound of a guitar and a harmonica played beside a railroad track at night. A fast freight goes by, and while them cars are rushin' along, you can't hear that lonesome whistle—you hear the music again. It ain't never stopped. It ain't never gonna stop."

The music of my land sometimes is obscured by the tumult and shouting of groups in conflict, muted by recession and unemployment. But there is a symphonic background of love and truth, beauty and freedom, that "ain't never gonna stop." It broods over millions of homes wherein faith and love abide and sings in the integrity of men and women who honor the marts of trade with their courage. It can be heard above "the noise of selfish strife" in the compassion of multitudes who care for the welfare of others.

13

There is an underlying love of freedom in my land, nourished by memories of pilgrims, patriots, and pioneers. None can abridge the right of the loyal opposition to speak in protest against the plans and programs of men in power. No one can thwart the right of any other to "life, liberty, and the pursuit of happiness." Careers are open to the talented, and no one within the law can be compelled against his will. We write as we please, speak as we please, worship as we please, and think as we please.

When my land is threatened by moral sag, there is a sustaining strength in the fibers of men and women who are unwilling to buckle under. The white spires of churches in a thousand towns and villages are reminders that the sources of our freedom are spiritual. The Gothic towers of churches on our Main Streets call us to renewed concern for the values that undergird our common life. We are a people "under God," and deep down we know it.

Amidst the din and clatter of factories, mills, and mines, there is a camaraderie of creativity, initiative, and competence. The boredom of assembly lines cannot still the inner desire to build and to create. There is a latent pride in worthy workmanship that even computers cannot erase and a will to achievement that marks the workman worthy of his hire. These are sources of strength and promise for the land that I love.

If there are some who have despoiled the land we share, still the beauty of the land is beyond belief. There are towering mountain peaks festooned with snow that look down on fruited plains, where the clear streams from the mountains are tamed by canals and ditches to nourish the land. My land is blessed by fields of waving grain and the cattle on a thousand hills. It is made lovely by blue lakes, flowering deserts, and rockbound coasts.

When cynics carp and complain that the land I love is so decadent and beset by ills that it can't be saved, I still hear the music in the background. "It ain't never gonna stop."

Our Inheritance

"This is my own, my native land." It is a land of great traditions and glorious memories. It is a good land with resources that have nourished succeeding generations of innovators and inventors to whom we are debtors. We who share the present did not earn our inheritance. It is the gift of many who dreamed and labored through "peril, toil, and pain" to leave the land better than they found it.

We may be responsible, payers of taxes, conscientious, patriotic, and politically concerned, as we ought to be, but the land we cherish is ours because others labored before we came. "The land was ours," Robert Frost wrote in "The Gift Outright," "before we were the land's." The things we treasure most—the freedom, the ideals, the valued institutions, the faith that sustains us—were given, not earned.

The ideals of our native land have been framed in great phrases: "government by consent of the governed," "a nation of laws," "under God," and "in God we trust." Such statements and phrases, rooted in our inheritance, are by no means outmoded. They are sources of our strength as a nation, to be cherished and celebrated in our time of trouble.

If, as has been widely suggested, there has been a breakdown of the old order, it is because we have been careless, forgetting that the gifts from the past, like the hinges on old gates, grow rusty from neglect. While we have been in the throes of a revolution of change and threatened decay, we have discounted the past and overlooked the powers of renewal implicit in our inheritance from the generations that have passed.

One of the tragedies of our time has been the unreflective,

mindless reactions and decisions that have been devoid of reference to our inheritance. The ironic conformisms of the rebels and the dropouts, following the fads, are as mindless as the conformisms of exponents of the status quo.

We were born to be free, free "under God," with due respect for righteousness, truth, and human dignity. We are free to be faddists, who follow the "in" things of the hour, but we are accountable for the consequences in our common life. We are free to be Archie Bunkers, bigots to the core, but we are responsible for the results of our bigotry. We should be aware that, as either conformists or bigots, we are at odds with our inheritance.

We sing of "liberty in law," which suggests we are ruled by laws rather than by the whims of parties or men. It should be noted, however, that the free man's morality does not emerge from fear of the law, but rather from the deeps of his own commitment to God in whom he lives and moves and has his being. His ideals and values command his obedience to standards far higher than those demanded by the law.

Our great experiment in democracy surely will erode unless we renew our faith that "God is our ruler yet," undergirding our highest ideals and aspirations with His strength, faith that our integrity rests its weight on His grace. Our struggles for justice find their dynamic in His deep caring for individual men and women; our loyalty to truth achieves its power because He is the truth. Our great traditions, however betrayed, are founded on the righteousness of God.

We are most free, not when we are simply doing what we please, scornful of laws and indifferent toward ideals that lift us above the law, but rather when we are committed to God and guided by sound learning and honest piety. We are free when the inner spiritual constraints of our faith sustain our integrity and lead us so to love our fellowmen that we can be neither unjust nor unfair in our dealings with them.

We honor the inheritance that is ours in this "land of the free and the home of the brave" when, as individuals, we cherish and preserve for the generations yet to be, the high ideals and ultimate values that flow from our faith in God. "This is my own, my native land," given to my care and yours to love, honor, and protect for our children and theirs.

Some Diviner Mold

It was something of a shock when a singing group in Aspen, Colorado, announced in humorous song in the midst of our bicentennial, "I'm tired of seventy-six." It seemed a little premature to be weary of remembering our glorious past. Nevertheless, the theme of the song seems appropriate now. It appeared to be saying, "Let's be done with celebrating the past and get on with the future."

Having remembered the beginnings of the nation in song, pageantry, and speeches, it is time to think of tomorrow and the day after. John Greenleaf Whittier must have been thinking in that vein when he wrote in the last lines of his "Centennial Hymn," written for the opening of the International Exhibition in Philadelphia in 1876:

> And, cast in some diviner mold,
> Let the new cycle shame the old!

However great the past may have been, "some diviner mold" is required for the future.

In many ways, our achievements have shamed the past. The nation is rich beyond the dreams of Midas. It is mighty in its military power, vital in its industrial development and scientific genius. The "new cycle" is testimony to the ingenuity and initiative of the nation's people. Whether the years following 1776 and 1876 were cast in "a diviner mold," however, is open to question.

The "diviner mold" cannot be measured in terms of the things we possess, the gadgets that make life easier, the automobiles that are better and more expensive, or the televisions and radios that

17

make us privy to world events as they happen. These suggest only that we cherish things that are the means for living. They say nothing about our concern, or lack of it, for the ends of life.

What we will make of the years to come will depend not on our wealth or power, but rather on the purposes that infuse our lives with meaning and significance. Those who signed the Declaration of Independence risked "their lives, their fortunes, and their sacred honor" for the right of every man to seek "life, liberty, and the pursuit of happiness" on his own terms. Their lives were infused with a purpose that enabled them to endure defeat and failure, discouragement and hardship, on the road to triumph.

It is the intangible rather than the tangible, the eternal, not the temporal, that gives meaning to struggle and makes life worth living. Life is dull when the days vanish without a trace of any purpose accomplished, and hours slip away unlived. When we care too little to throw our weight behind some vision of what should be, we are tired not only of 1976 but also of life itself.

The "diviner mold" for tomorrow challenges us to revive the flagging ethical vitality of the nation; to risk our lives, our fortunes, and our sacred honor for principles in which we believe; to speak with honest words only; to act from decent motives purely; and to live with unadulterated integrity. What happens in Washington, the seat of power, or in the councils of our cities, will hinge on the quality of our personal concern for moral values.

When we are tempted to say, "What I do doesn't matter," we forget that every violation of decency and honor weakens the fabric of the society we share. Every evidence of moral courage, of living for the worthiest things of earth, gives strength to the whole and nourishes the inner strength of the nation. Whenever a man or a woman stands up to challenge injustice or wrong, the faith of the community and the nation is fed. If the nation blunders into decadence, our children may ask in the years to come, "Where were you when this was coming to pass?"

The "diviner mold" will be the issue of our ethical commitment and our spiritual renewal. When we can say honestly, "In God we trust," the dynamic of moral purpose will follow; our lives will find new meaning; and the "new cycle" will "shame the old."

Before 1776

In our bicentennial year of 1976, we were grateful for the patriots who gathered in Philadelphia in 1776 to declare the independence of the thirteen colonies from Great Britain. It should be noted, however, that those who affirmed their rights to "life, liberty, and the pursuit of happiness" were heirs of a growing spirit of independence, initiative, and self-government.

The Pilgrims who landed at Plymouth in 1620 formed "a civil body politick" and swore loyalty to the government they had framed "in the name of God." Forty-one heads of families signed the "Compact of the Pilgrims," the first instrument of civil government ever subscribed to by all the people concerned.

Few suspected that the Mayflower Compact, as it came to be known, would mark the beginning of a new nation "with liberty and justice for all." Nevertheless, the seeds of the future were planted when the Pilgrims affixed their names to a document "by Vertue hereof to enact, constitute, and frame such just and equal lawes, ordinances, Acts, Constitutions & Offices, from Time to Time, as shall be thought most mete & convenient for the generall good of the Colonie, unto which we promise all due submission and obedience."

Years later, Henry Wadsworth Longfellow gave voice to the meaning of the Pilgrim venture in the name of freedom when he wrote:

> Down to the Plymouth rock, that had been to their feet
>   as a doorstep,
> Into a world unknown—the corner stone of a nation.

While the Pilgrims affirmed their loyalty to England and the

King, they also laid foundations for self-government "under God" and for the ultimate independence of the nation.

Almost half of the 102 *Mayflower* passengers who came to the new land perished during the first winter. Nevertheless, in 1621, Governor William Bradford decreed a day of Thanksgiving to be celebrated when the first corn crop had been gathered. When the day came, tables were set outdoors, and more than a score of friendly Indians, bringing venison and wild turkeys from the woods, joined the celebration.

Significantly, the first Thanksgiving was not simply a feast. It was infinitely more. There were prayers and songs of praise, sermons, and the reciting of Psalms, as if the loyalty and gratitude of the Pilgrims belonged to God alone. They were saved by "the grace of God" and by their own courage, ingenuity, and faith.

With the passing of time, the Thanksgiving custom spread from Plymouth to other colonies. Governors issued Thanksgiving Day proclamations, as if to affirm that the roots of freedom and national health are spiritual. During the American Revolution, eight special days of thanks were observed, and President George Washington issued a general proclamation for a day of thanks in 1789.

Deep in the heart of the emerging nation was the conviction that, as Washington said, "every step by which we have advanced to the character of an independent nation seems to have been distinguished by some token of Providential Agency." That faith stemmed from the heritage of Plymouth and was plowed into the culture of the nation.

So it is that we continue to give thanks to God, not for the feast of Thanksgiving Day, but rather for the God-given dignity and significance of human personality on which our freedom rests and for whatever "token[s] of Providential Agency" have sustained and guided us through the nation's crises.

Those who wrested farms from the wilderness and fashioned tools from their own forges, elected councils, and built schools for their children and churches to sustain their faith have provided us with an inheritance of independence, ingenuity, and courageous faith that is worth preserving. Their faith in their Creator was the substance of their courage and their strength to survive. They offered their thanks because they knew God's grace was the foundation of their achievements.

Tempered by Tenacity

In "Western Star," Stephen Vincent Benét pictures the Pilgrims who stayed behind when their comrades departed in the *Mayflower*. It was on September 16, 1620, that the *Mayflower* sailed after two false starts. The *Speedwell*, the second ship the Pilgrims expected would take them to the New World, leaked badly. She was overmasted and had to be abandoned. There was, therefore, no room for a score or more who had planned to make the voyage.

Thinking things over, there were some who elected not to go. They returned to London, and when they got there

> Felt, doubtless, that queer blend of relief and shame
> Which comes to those who make sensible decisions.

Quite possibly they were not really committed to the voyage, and, when an easy way out appeared, they availed themselves of it. Of course, they rationalized their decision.

> And yet one wonders,
> What they thought later.

They were safe, but they missed one of the great sagas of history.

Like those who remained behind, we often turn back too soon from the ventures of our lives and miss the greatness we might find if we dared to

> Go on forever and fail and go on again,
> To be mauled to earth and arise . . .

in the spirit of Robert Louis Stevenson, a gallant prince of life, or the Pilgrims who sailed for the New World.

When times are out of joint and our hopes are dimmed by the moral equivalent of a leaky ship, it is easy to give up the battle and surrender to inertia. Mauled to earth by forces beyond our

21

control, we conclude that the fates are against us and retreat into resentment and bitterness. When jobs are scarce, why go on endlessly failing to find a place where our talents can be used? Why go on banging our heads against a stone wall?

Those of us who lived through the agony of the Great Depression know full well what hardship and discouragement mean. The struggle to survive was very real, and the future seemed "black as the pit from pole to pole." There were many who lost both faith and hope and never came back to achieve the promise of their lives. There were others who, like Beethoven facing deafness, "seized fate by the throat" and refused to quit.

St. John Ervine says of George Bernard Shaw that "his gay courage and his fortitude in adversity have resulted in a widespread belief that he never felt despondent when times were hard and manuscripts unerringly returned." The fact is that Shaw refused to yield to bitterness and went on writing despite poverty and disappointment. If he had a watchword, it may well have been the sentence he applied to the hero of one of his early novels, "The power to stand alone is worth acquiring at the expense of much sorrowful solitude."

We learn to stand alone and to develop whatever capacities we have, not when things are going well, but rather when we are being tested in the fires of adversity. As Paul, the apostle, wrote, "Rejoice in tribulation, for tribulation worketh patience, and patience worketh experience, and experience hope."

When our ships seem to be leaking and the voyages of our lives frustrated, it is time not to yield to despair, but rather to seek within ourselves the untapped riches of mind and spirit that can see us through tribulation to patience and hope. Veterans of the Klondike gold rush were forever telling stories of fabulous gold mines abandoned by their original seekers just before hidden lodes would have been reached. The riches were left untapped until others came and dug deeper. Often it is so in our own experience.

It requires a high quality of faith in God and in ourselves to press on with hope and courage when we are beset by frustration and discouragement. Nevertheless, without faith to push on, we never discover the untapped riches in ourselves. What is more, concerning those disposed to turn back and give up, one wonders what they will think later.

Might in Little Things

In the early days of the American Revolution, things went badly for George Washington and his ill-trained army. Ill-equipped, inadequately led, and poorly trained, the army suffered repeated defeats. Washington was severely criticized, even though no one could have done more with the officers and troops at the command of the brave Virginian.

While Washington struggled to build an army worthy of the name, Major General Charles Lee, who had hoped to be named Commander in Chief, did what he could to undermine Washington. He refused to bring the troops under his command, the most experienced and best-equipped men in the Continental Army, to join the battered troops of Washington.

Richard M. Ketchum, in his fine book *The Winter Soldiers,* wrote that Lee was "vain and ambitious . . . was profane, a heavy drinker, a womanizer, and a man who delighted in dirty stories." He was "scornful of Washington's habit of constantly deferring to Congress, and he had little use for the principle of military subservience to a civilian government."

If Lee had not dallied over breakfast one morning in a farmhouse a mile or two from the troops he commanded, he would not have been ingloriously captured by the British. He might very well have become the Commander in Chief of the Continental Army. Ketchum notes that "from the vantage point of hindsight, it is just conceivable that his disappearance from center stage may have been the luckiest possible break for the country."

Little things may be significant, not so much in themselves, but because they often involve matters of large consequence. Charles Lee might have become the man on horseback with too much authority, and if he had, the future of the nation would have been far different. He loved power; Washington did not. A small matter, like dallying over breakfast, turned out to be of major importance.

Important events often hang on slender threads, and decisive issues are influenced by trifles. Sir Alexander Fleming was intrigued by a plate of spoiled culture. The blue-green mold that appeared inspired his curiosity. He wrote in his notebook, "I was sufficiently interested in the antibacterial substance produced by the mold to pursue the subject." What he found on investigation he called "penicillin."

Too often, I suspect, we ignore or overlook the little things that can make a large difference. Charles Lee's short moment of carelessness and self-indulgence cost him his career and changed the course of United States history. Napoleon met disaster at Waterloo because he did not know that a sunken road stood in the path of his army.

Little things often make the difference between success and failure. Marriages frequently come to grief for lack of concern for small matters. The appreciative word unsaid, the small courtesy neglected, the little encouragement not given, all add up to the beginning of marital disintegration. We usually can manage big troubles together. It is the little things that throw us.

Men and women of stature and great usefulness got where they are, not by ignoring trifles, but by recognizing the significance in small things others missed. They understood the importance of the little more that is so much, and they gave it with relish. They were alert to the small opportunities and made the most of them. When others were careless, they were precise.

It was Michelangelo who said, "Little things make perfection, and perfection is no trifle." Washington would not have won the battles of Trenton, Princeton, or Yorktown without infinite care for details. The perfection of his plans was no trifle.

Both individual life and history often turn on little things, the little more or the little less attention to detail, carelessness or precision, and patience or the absence of it.

Nation Makers

In the perspective of history, it is something of a miracle that the thirteen colonies got together, fought a successful war against Britain, formed a Constitution for the nation, and managed to make it work. Members of the First Continental Congress differed bitterly over policies to cope with what was viewed as English tyranny. As John Adams noted years later of those who shared colonial life, "one-third were Tories, one-third Whigs, and the rest mongrels."

The Constitutional Convention of 1787 brought together men of mixed motives and concerns. They were not, for the most part, pure idealists wearing halos. On the contrary, they were practical men with conflicting interests. James Madison was realistically honest when he insisted that good government could be based only on "ambition countering ambition." Asked by a mocking delegate if he were saying that "the frailties of human nature are the proper elements of good government," Madison replied, "I know no other."

When the Constitution was adopted, it reflected the conviction that man's idealism often is corrupted by his interests and his principles are undermined by his ambition and his desire for power. While Madison and his colleagues hoped for the best in human behavior, they designed a document that would guard against the worst.

It is a tribute to the quality of colonial leadership that the nation's Constitution was fashioned and adopted. An abler body of men probably never has met in the United States. George Washington was elected president of the Constitutional Convention. Among the delegates were James Madison, Edmund Randolph, Benjamin Franklin, Rufus King, Roger Sherman, and Alexander Hamilton.

James Madison was the great innovator. He clearly perceived the situation as it was and sensed the direction in which the new nation should move. An ardent student of the past, he accepted the Age of Reason concept that "the past should enlighten us on the future: knowledge of history is no more than anticipated experience. . . . Where we see the same faults followed regularly by the same misfortunes, we may reasonably think that, if we could have known the first, we might have avoided the others." With his understanding of history, Madison was able to foresee the unforeseeable and to guard against it.

It was George Washington, whose genius and courage had pulled the colonists through the agonies of war, who stood as the symbol of unity in the midst of diversity and difference. His voice seldom was heard in the Convention, but his wisdom and quiet influence were vital. He trusted Madison and supported the strong union advocated by Hamilton and Madison.

Benjamin Franklin was the voice of conciliation and necessary compromise. He understood well that politics is the art of the possible, and, with eloquence and power, he pleaded for adoption of the Constitution, whatever its faults or limitations, as a sound foundation for the new nation. Franklin's final address to the Convention gave the final push for the adoption of the Constitution. He said: "I confess that I do not entirely approve of this Constitution, at present. . . . In these sentiments, Sir, I agree to this Constitution, with all its faults, if such they are; because I think a general Government necessary for us and there is no form of government but what may be a blessing to the people if well administered." He affirmed his conviction that the Constitution would be well administered and would fail only "when the people shall become so corrupted as to need despotic government, being incapable of any other."

The Constitution has served us well through 200 years, and we can be grateful to the men who nurtured its birth. It will serve us well so long as we cherish both our freedom and the responsibilities it entails. The foundations of the past are sound, and on them new leaders will build and lead us through the ills of the present to a better tomorrow. As William Stafford wrote, "Somewhere there must be a next achievement, maybe tomorrow."

Stand Beside Her

When Arthur Fiedler led the audience in singing "God Bless America" at one of his pop concerts, men and women stood spontaneously and sang with reverent enthusiasm. As the television camera swept the audience, it caught an elderly man wiping away a tear, a young woman whose lower lip quivered with emotion as she sang, and a youngster standing on his seat and singing as if his future depended on God's guidance of the nation.

The song that night took on the aspects of a prayer for the land we love, a prayer for God to "stand beside her and guide her" through the shoals of a difficult time. Possibly, if God "holds the whole world in His hands," there is room in those hands for our land and its people. Surely the nation needs God to "stand beside her and guide her" now and in the days to come.

The spiritual yearning implicit in the way we sing "God Bless America" suggests not only an awareness of our need for God but also a deep underlying faith in God. We are not an irreligious people. On the contrary, our spiritual inheritance is deeply interfused in our thought and emotions. We cannot altogether escape the conviction that we are dependent on a Power beyond ourselves in whose hands our destiny rests.

We know our land has been blessed abundantly "from the mountains, to the prairies, to the oceans, white with foam." The majestic mountains, etched with snow and flowered with whispering pines and the glory of rustling aspen trees, feed the river valleys born to nourish the plains. And how the prairies blossom with ripening grain, corn "as high as an elephant's eye," milo turning rust-brown, and wheat waving in the sun!

Beneath the good earth of our land, a wealth of coal awaits both our digging and the science and technology to use it to fuel our factories and replace foreign supplies of oil. We are not without God-given resources to meet the needs of our land. It is only the will and the plans that we lack.

We have people resources, too—the young people of our land—free, as nowhere else on earth, to use their talents and develop their skills. They come to the nation's schools and colleges from the "hollers" of Appalachia and the ghettos of our cities, from the farms and the ranches, and from the suburbs and the small towns of our land. They march in endless processions to be graduated from great universities and small colleges. How well they use their learning depends on them.

Our national memories, if they are plowed into the minds of the generation coming on, have the power to save us from the tyranny of the few and keep our freedoms secure. The Founding Fathers served us well when they linked our liberty to spiritual values anchored in God and fashioned documents to secure "life, liberty, and the pursuit of happiness" for all who share the land we love.

We have sculptured the great moments of our past in bronze and stone, from Concord Bridge to Appomattox and from Constitution Hall to Williamsburg, "lest we forget." In literature and in song, we are reminded of the providence of God in our history, and we yearn now for "intimations of the Invisible" to "stand beside" us and "guide" us through the days to come.

In our most thoughtful moments, we plead for wisdom for ourselves and for our leaders. Our problems seem too great for small minds unenlightened by "the light from above," too vast to be met by niggardly aims that center in our selfish interests, and too overwhelming without the selfless spirit of men and women willing to risk their "lives, their fortunes, and their sacred honor" for the common good of the land. To acknowledge in mind and spirit that we are "under God" is our hope.

So it is that we pray in song and in words for our land, its people, and its leaders. It is our faith that our land is in God's hands and that He will "stand beside her and guide her."

Our Goodly Heritage

I, who have seen the storm ride down the sky,
Heavy with ghosts and shadows and dead dreams,
Still see one ray of light that will not die,
One star that gleams.

This is the star called Courage that must shine
If the old world we know may hold its place
In the vast march of planets, line on line,
Through endless space.

"Beyond the Storm" by GRANTLAND RICE

Worthy to Be Free

James Madison and his colleagues who wrote the Constitution were both realistic and positive. They viewed human nature with healthy skepticism as they labored on the document that came from the Constitutional Convention of 1787. James Bryce noted that the Constitution "is the work of men who believed in original sin and were resolved to leave open for transgressors no door which they could possibly shut."

No doubt John Calvin would have approved the Constitution. He had no illusions concerning the nature of man, the fallen creature who needed to be saved from himself. The Founding Fathers were decisively influenced by Calvin as they struggled to protect the new nation from the sinful propensities of men. As Viscount Bryce suggested, "The aim of the Constitution seems to be not so much to attain great common ends by securing good government as to avert the evils which will flow not merely from a bad government but from any government strong enough to threaten existing communities and individual citizens."

The idea of centralized power disturbed Madison and his colleagues, even though they understood the necessity for a government strong enough to be effective. Essentially, they mistrusted men who might be elected to positions of power or who, by virtue of wealth or influence, might be able to subvert the government.

Thomas Paine, unjustly described by Theodore Roosevelt as "a dirty little atheist," was a thoroughgoing Calvinist when he wrote, "Society is the fruit of our virtues, but government is the product of our wickedness." He understood that a government strong enough to deal with the wickedness of men was necessary.

History has justified the fears of the Constitution makers that corruptible human nature corrupts government. The system of checks and balances that they wrote into the Constitution was designed to guard the nation against the ambitions of the unscrupulous. Their idealism was balanced by an honest realism about human nature.

The checks and balances in the Constitution frequently make governing difficult. When Congress and the President are at odds and the Supreme Court disposed at one time to be liberal and at other times conservative, the government appears to be devoid of the power to act. Nevertheless, as Winston Churchill noted, "Democracy is the worst form of government ever invented, except for every other."

What stands clear now, as in the early days of the nation's history, is the need for incorruptible men and women in every area of our common life. Democracy always is threatened by the corrupt and the dishonest. It is saved by men and women who cannot be bought or coerced by favors offered by those in positions of power. Its strength is in a consensus of ideals and values in the body politic.

Ralph Waldo Emerson was haunted by the absence of commitment to ideals and values and by the "hollowness of heart" in those who shared the nation he knew and loved. "Genuine belief has left us. The underlying principles of the States are not honestly believed in," he lamented. "The depravity of the business classes of our country is not less than has been supposed, but infinitely greater."

What troubled Emerson most was the lack of motivating beliefs strong enough to make men and women worthy to be free. A similar concern troubles the thoughtful of our time. Only a motivating faith in God can create incorruptible men and women committed to honesty and integrity, justice and righteousness. Nothing less than high religion can sustain the courage and honor of men and women in politics, in business, or in the professions. Essentially, we are what we believe.

The authors of the Constitution provided safeguards to protect us against the unscrupulous; they could not make us fit to bear the burdens of our own freedom. Nothing less than worthy religion can do that.

Freedom and Responsibility

To those of us who believe in freedom, it is disturbing to notice that two-thirds or more of the people in the developing countries appear to be willing to exchange freedom for order or for order in tandem with economic growth and national prestige. The assumption seems to be that progress requires ultimate external restraint and coercion to limit the freedom of men to speak and act as individuals.

We in the Western world have inherited faith in freedom, a firm belief that progress comes as a result of individual initiative and struggle. Traditionally, we have assumed that, in the providence of God, reason will triumph over unreason, sense over nonsense, and truth over falsehood. We have been willing to risk the interplay of competitive forces with a minimum of external regulation.

Now and then we have doubted our own faith, wondering if law and order could be maintained in a free society. Under stress, we have been tempted to exchange freedom for order, as if freedom might be too great a luxury to be endured in a disrupted society. At the moment, we seem to be uncertain of ourselves. Arthur Bremer, who shot and wounded former Governor George Wallace, suggested a disturbing mood when he remarked, "I would have liked it if society had protected me from myself."

In the past, society has sought to protect us from ourselves with moral sanctions, established conventions simply perceived and accepted by consensus. Essentially, the word *morality* meant "mores," meaning customs or social regulations. To be sure, even those standards of behavior accepted by consensus often were violated, but the violations were recognized as violations. The mores of society imposed restraints that helped to protect us from our own impulses to disregard social taboos.

Morality, however, has a second meaning, one valued in Christian thought and in the thought of other great religions, namely, that morality is a matter of the spirit. Socrates called it "integrity of soul." It goes beyond customs or social regulations and involves inner integrity, respect for the rights of others, and caring concern for persons. It is only as society helps to inspire inner integrity in persons that society is able to protect us more adequately from ourselves and to undergird social order.

The upshot of the matter can be put in the words of Edmund Burke, who wrote: "Men are qualified for civil liberties in exact proportion to their disposition to put moral chains on their own appetites. . . . Society cannot exist unless a controlling power upon will and appetite be placed somewhere, and the less of it there is within, the more there must be without. It is ordained in the internal constitution of things that men of intemperate minds cannot be free. Their passions forge their fetters."

Unless we are able to "put moral chains" on our own appetites in such fashion that we are protected from ourselves, and so provide protection for society, we will be more and more disposed to trade freedom for order. If we are tempted to shy away from the idea of "moral chains," let me suggest that the only such chains I mean are those that are inwardly imposed by the demands of our own integrity of mind and spirit.

The weakening of the inner "moral chains" that protect both ourselves and society has been coincident with the decline of religion in our time. Having forsaken both Sinai and Calvary as symbols of the highest, we have undermined the ethical foundations on which freedom rests. If we wish both freedom and order, we will need to affirm once again, "In God we trust."

Liberty in Law

It is important to notice that laws and codes of behavior compose the necessary framework for freedom and order. The truth of the matter is suggested in a verse from "America the Beautiful":

> America, America,
> God mend thine every flaw,
> Confirm thy soul in self-control,
> Thy liberty in law.

Athenian liberty died, Lord Acton wrote, because its age possessed no fixed standards of right and wrong. Ethical values had no abiding authority, and, as a consequence, Athens fell into decadence. Freedom foundered because it lost the framework "in law" that had undergirded it.

Unfortunately, we have been blundering into a similar wasteland in which our ethical values have been called into question. In a discussion of contemporary literature, Edmund Fuller noted what he called "the decline of the sense of good and evil in many of our writers." He went on to say that "the idea that there is neither good nor evil in any absolute moral or religious sense is widespread in our times." In short, we are where the Greeks were before the decline of Athenian liberty.

I do not mean to say that our society necessarily is on a toboggan toward disaster, but I do mean to suggest we cannot afford to undermine the authority of the Ten Commandments and ignore ethical and religious codes of behavior. Loyalty to a code, the Ten Commandments, for example, does not guarantee that the right things will be done in every case. On the other hand, it does insure that one who acts in obedience to the code will do the right thing much more often than if he acted from instinct or private intuition.

On one occasion, Adlai Stevenson, speaking of a politician of particularly rancid practices, said: "If he were a bad man, I wouldn't be so afraid of him. But this man has no principles. He doesn't know the difference." The question for our society is simply this: Are we losing the capacity to tell the difference between right and wrong, good and evil? Ideals and rules, codes and standards, have fallen away in large chunks under the impact of "The Secular City."

Robert Frost, with his usual perception, sensed the way our ethical fences are being cut. He wondered why man's nature has stubbornly remained

> ...forever so hard to teach
> That though there is no fixed line between wrong and right,
> There are roughly zones whose laws must be obeyed.

That is to say, codes, laws, and rules never are entirely adequate to meet our ethical dilemmas. Nevertheless, they are helpful guidelines. And, if Aristotle was right in saying there are many ways of doing wrong but only one way of doing what is right, we need all the guidance we can get if we are to find the right. Simple hunches are not enough.

It should be noted, however, that legal correctness and respectability are minimum or proximate values. We are in need of something more than the coercion of codes or customs, laws or rules, because we can't seem to stay within the boundaries set by ethical fences. It is true, as Paul Tillich wrote, "Our moral balance sheet is not so bad as it might be." On the other hand, it is not nearly so good as it could be.

Freedom in Crisis

There is a widespread disposition to assume that freedom means being released from all regularities, exploring borderlands around ethical rules. There are times when we seem to measure the scope of our freedom by the size of the dump containing our discarded inhibitions. Our standards, like our automobiles, are relegated to the refuse heap because they are old.

Real freedom, however, is positive. It is not mere liberation from restraint or standards. It is freedom for something. Essentially, it is freedom to be and to do what in our finest hours we know we ought to be and do. We are free, not when we are at liberty to do as we please, but when we are able to do as we ought.

Socrates was convinced there was in himself what he called a "daimon" who spoke directly to him, calling him to an obedience to the best he knew. We would call it conscience, an inward monitor. Socrates was not free to do as he pleased. He was free, however, to do as he ought.

We are told in a moving passage in the *Crito* how Socrates, on the eve of his death, refused to make his escape from prison, even after his friends had made all the necessary arrangements. He had been imprisoned unjustly, but he imagined the laws of the city as standing before him in visible form and commanding him to remain. He was free to escape except for something in himself. The laws of the city reminded him of how they had done everything for him, from the hour of his birth and before it. Now that the law had condemned him, he would not debase its authority in order to gain for himself a few years of wretched life.

Freedom flourishes in the mind and heart, in man's capacity to be himself at his best. Paul, the apostle, in prison, Sir Walter

37

Raleigh in the tower, John Bunyan in Bedford jail, John Huss and the Maid of Orleans at the stake were more free than their accusers and jailers. They were free to affirm their faith, their beliefs, and their deepest convictions despite circumstances. If they had abandoned their convictions under pressure, they would not have been free.

Our discarded inhibitions and abandoned standards suggest, not that we are more free than we once were, but that we are less free. We have been coerced by contemporary culture to do as the Romans do and to shout with the voices of conforming slaves, "Don't fence me in." The voice of the inward monitor we call conscience has been muted by the huge army of the world's desires.

The challenge of freedom is that we be masters of our own fate, not victims of the pressures that overwhelm the "daimon" calling us to higher ground. It takes the courage of the free to plan a purposeful life and to live with a sense of both identity and dignity. If freedom means anything, it means liberty to be ourselves at our best, no matter what circumstances stand in our way.

Positive freedom is our hope, freedom to stand sun-crowned above the corruptions of earth, to affirm our faith in the sacredness of human life, and to work for justice and compassion in human affairs. If there are times when we pray in the words of G. K. Chesterton's hymn "O God of Earth and Altar":

> O God of earth and altar,
> Bow down and hear our cry,
> Our earthly rulers falter,
> Our people drift and die,

we will neither falter nor drift because we are free to stand for the best in our common life.

The democracy we cherish is not a society in which each man demands the right to do as he happens to please. It is a society of men and women free to do and be as they ought to do and be. What is more, it is a society in which each man and woman demands that other persons be allowed to be and do as they ought. This implies, of course, that the inner monitor sets limits on our own liberty. The future hinges on the positive freedom we exercise in our life together.

What Is Honored Here?

The Madison Avenue portrait of comfort and ease to come in the scientific millennium before us leaves me wishing for the quiet of Walden Pond with Henry David Thoreau. In the future, so the Madison Avenue ads suggest, microwaves will cook our food and laser beams will disintegrate the household garbage. Ultrasonic waves will replace water for dishwashing. The house curtains will be self-cleaning, and never-wear aluminum floors will minimize domestic labors.

One might go on listing the mechanical labor-saving gadgets designed to make our lives easier. The assumption of the Madison Avenue predictions is that we will have enough energy to keep our gadgets functioning. Be that as it may, if the advertisers are correct, we seem to be intent on making life comfortable with the scientific equivalent of silk cushions.

After considering the possibilities of these comforts, I was reminded of Plato's observation that "what is honored in a country will be cultivated there." If we honor comfort and ease, these will be fostered in our culture. Even now, we substitute golf carts for exercise and TV athletic events for participation. Electronic calculators take the labor out of math.

Whether we like it or not, we are creatures of values. We regard some things in life as desirable—to be sought, cultivated, encouraged, and strengthened. Others we are inclined to avoid, downgrade, or even destroy. Who wants to strain and struggle in a culture that values ease? If we can be comfortable on food stamps and get along on government subsidies, why should we bother to push ourselves?

Democratic society, however, depends on men and women who

are willing to exert themselves on behalf of something more significant than personal comfort. As André Gide wrote, "He who has only himself for his goal, has a void." We are free to choose our goals and our commitments, but our destiny hinges on the objectives we choose.

The Rockefeller Panel reports, entitled "Prospect for America," summarize the goals of a free society in noting that "the conviction is that the value of all human arrangements must be measured by what they do to enhance the life of the individual—to help him grow in knowledge, sensitivity, and the mastery of himself and his destiny. The faith is that the individual has the capacity to meet this challenge."

While the panel reports focus the goal of democratic society in the individual, their thrust is to impose on the individual the obligation to "grow in knowledge, sensitivity," and self-mastery and to impose on society the obligation to make such growth possible within the context of its institutions. This is by no means an invitation to be comfortable. It is rather a challenge to grow.

The assumption of a free society is that the best people, that is, those who are knowledgeable, sensitive, self-controlled, and ethically rooted, are the best citizens. They infuse the institutions of society with the ideals and values they cherish and so make possible the development of individuals who qualify as the best people. They are what Jesus called "the salt of the earth," flavoring the life and thinking of their time.

It is worth remembering what Thomas Jefferson once wrote to John Adams: "I agree with you that there is a natural aristocracy among men. The grounds of this are virtue and talents." He went on to suggest that such men should be elected to the offices of government. Jefferson believed fervently in democracy, but he was aware of the need for the best people to infuse their ideals into the operation of government institutions.

Plato's observation, therefore, is of the utmost importance: "What is honored in a country will be cultivated there." If we honor men and women of "virtue and talents" we will cultivate such. If we honor those who are merely comfortable and at ease, we will cultivate listless and easy-going people. If we honor men and women of knowledge, sensitivity, and self-mastery, we will nurture a generation of men and women worthy to be free.

Past—Present—Perhaps

Looking back across the busy years, memories crowd into consciousness to remind us how the world has changed. Only yesterday, horses and buggies cluttered dusty, unpaved streets and news of important events came to us by way of newsboys shouting, "Extra, Extra!" The world moved slowly and the horseless carriage was a rarity. Trolley cars moved along the city streets unimpeded by traffic jams.

Clumsy telephones, with cranks to call Central, clung to walls, and electric lights were dim. When the women cleaned house, they wrapped their heads in towels and swept with brooms. Dust clouds filled the rooms they swept, and dust had to be wiped from furniture and shelves. Now, with our gadgets and labor-saving devices, it is difficult to recapture the mood of that day.

Neighborhoods were neighborly, and friends from next door or up the street popped in and out. Nobody locked doors, and the streets were safe. It was normal to stroll in the parks at night without fear. Families stuck together, with children, their parents, and a grandparent or two composing the household. There was discipline both at home and at school, where moral values were emphasized.

In time, Henry Ford put the nation on wheels. The old Model T had some limitations. It was a chore spinning the crank to get it going with the thermometer at 5 below zero, and not exactly pleasant driving with no heater and flapping side-curtains to keep out the worst of the wind and cold. A flat tire meant changing it yourself, patching the puncture, and then pumping it up with a hand pump. Driving a Model T required muscle!

There are many things about "the good old days" we would

41

not invite back if we could. The memories are pleasant, viewed through the haze of distance, but we would not exchange today for yesterday. With all the ills of today, we would not go back to horses and buggies, Model T Fords, brooms, unpaved streets, and newsboys shouting. We much prefer the present, with television and radio, heated automobiles with self-starters, vacuum cleaners, and electric ovens.

There are some things, though, that we might well recover from the past: the sense of family solidarity, discipline, idealism, a sense of national purpose, and faith to live by. These never are outdated or passé. They do not lose their value like Model T Fords or high-button shoes. They give us a sense of direction and meaning in life. They still remain valid for a nation that has been industrialized, computerized, and organized to satisfy our needs and whims.

The comment of Thomas Huxley more than 100 years ago after a visit to the United States remains relevant: "I cannot say that I am in the slightest degree impressed by your bigness and your material resources as such. Size is not grandeur and territory does not make a nation. The great issue about which hangs the terror of overhanging fate is: 'What are you doing with all these things?' " This is the question we must confront today.

What we do with what we have depends on the ideals and values we cherish and serve. Our wealth is not grandeur, and our labor-saving gadgets do not make a nation. Our greatness in the years to come will hinge on the renewal of our devotion to values and ideals the past has bequeathed to us. It rests, in the long run, on families wherein fair-minded discipline makes children into responsible citizens; on schools that inspire a love of learning and respect for the right; and on churches and synagogues that generate respect for the dignity of every individual as a child of God.

The road ahead is being charted today by our concern, or lack of concern, for principles that undergird our life together. Tomorrow is being fashioned in homes where children learn, or do not learn, to cherish integrity. The shape of the future is coming to be in our own commitment to responsible citizenship under God.

The great, overhanging question of our time is, Will we recover our grandeur as a nation dedicated to the values of our heritage?

Heritage of Fair Play

William James described the spirit of the nation's people as "the trained and disciplined good temper toward the other side when it fairly wins its inning." The idea of fair play is part of our American heritage, but, in our time, it seems to have been eroded both in sports and in public life.

Bottles and rolls of toilet paper thrown into sports arenas, often endangering baseball, hockey, or football players, suggest an erosion of sensitivity to fair play. Football quarterbacks deliberately injured and forced to the sidelines indicate a failure of "the trained and disciplined good temper toward the other side" in sports contests.

Winning is important, to be sure, but only on terms that are fair to both sides. Its importance is diminished when the means to victory defy the canons of decency and honor. It is better to lose with honor than to win with dishonor; it is better to lose an inning fairly than to win unfairly.

Such propositions appear to be under attack, not only in the arena of sports, but in other areas as well. The cartoon "Dunagin's People" suggested the truth. It portrayed a U.S. Military Academy cadet being admonished by the commanding general with the words, "Our strict honor code on cheating has been modified slightly . . . to don't get caught."

We need to remember, however, that our competitive system in sports, business, or education is based on fair play. Cheating or deception serves only to undermine the trust that makes the system work. We betray our heritage when we violate the rules, resort to trickery, or indulge in unfair methods. The system works effectively only when there is a consensus of belief that fair play is imperative, not elective.

Recent political campaigns suggest that apathy overwhelms the electorate when the candidates ignore vital issues and spend their time floating false rumors against their opponents and indulge in deception, if not downright dishonesty. When men or women running for offices betray their trust on the assumption that fairly winning an inning is less important than winning, they demean our heritage and destroy the trust that is vital for a free society.

Good temper and trust are inspired when one side "fairly wins its inning." Conflict, distrust, anger, and irritation are the result when winning comes from bribery, payoffs, deceitful claims, or dishonest presentations. There emerges a conviction that nobody can trust anybody, and this bodes ill for the future.

The undeniable truth is that "there is no right way to do a wrong thing"; there is no fair way to be foul. There is no honorable way to promise what cannot be delivered or to agree to do what cannot be accomplished. Foul means corrupt good ends, and dishonorable methods emasculate worthy goals. They betray the heritage on which our free society rests.

There is dignity in the wish to win on fair terms and to struggle against odds with honor unspoiled. Charles Darwin wrote in *The Descent of Man* that "the social instincts naturally lead to the Golden Rule, and this lies at the foundation of morality." Asking that we do unto others as we would have them do unto us, the Golden Rule is at the heart of fair play. It disdains taking unfair advantage of others.

Winning, and the popularity that goes with it, are heady stuff, but they are a spider's-web support for life that is easily destroyed by the realities of experience if we have unfairly won the inning and so undermined our heritage.

Great Expectations

Armistice Day, November 11, 1918, sticks in my memory. I was fourteen at the time, and, with my mother and father, I joined the deliriously happy mobs on the streets of Denver. It was like New Year's Eve in Times Square, except that there were tears of rejoicing in many eyes. The war was over, and the boys were coming home. If we did not "Hang the Kaiser," at least we would put him where he couldn't do any harm. We had won the war to end war and "to make the world safe for democracy," and it would be a wonderful world.

Somehow those great expectations were washed away by the wind and the tide. Winston Churchill was quite correct in saying that, after the war, "a vast fatigue dominated collective action." Old rivalries came to the surface, and the ideals expressed by Woodrow Wilson were emasculated by the interests of great powers intent on serving themselves.

Disenchantment inevitably follows the failure of great expectations. Much of the unrest of our time is rooted in disillusionment. The vast hopes of the black revolution of our day have been checkmated by economic and social realities. The ill-advised struggle in South Vietnam became a haunting frustration. Our spirits are fatigued as we struggle to pay our taxes and try to cope with social problems that seem too vast to yield to our efforts.

Quite possibly our great expectations have come to grief because somewhere we went off the spiritual and ethical track. William Butler Yeats noted the changed climate when he wrote that, in ancient times, men "looked as carefully and as patiently towards Sinai and its thunders as we look toward parliaments and laboratories." I have no wish to suggest that we abandon parliaments and laboratories in favor of chapels and churches, synagogues or cathedrals, but rather to propose that both laboratories and parliaments could do with greater ethical and spiritual commitments.

Churchill was right when he observed in 1929 that "without having improved appreciably in virtue or enjoying wiser guidance, mankind has got into its hands for the first time the tools by which it can unfailingly accomplish its own extermination." Our great expectations came to grief, not because we have been lacking in intellectual genius and mechanical know-how, but because we have been deficient in virtue and wiser guidance.

If the "thunders of Sinai" have been muted and the death of God announced, it is because we have come to the conclusion that what is required of us in our world of industrial might is not virtue, but competence, not reverence, but productivity. Institutions of our own creation serve our need for goods and services without the slightest by-your-leave of God. Why worry about virtue or wiser guidance when we have enough and more than we need of everything? Why not "worship the work of our own hands"?

It may be that we are beginning to wonder if perhaps we overlooked something. The "work of our own hands" has led us to crime on the streets, war, international monetary disruption, pollution of the air and water, and urban decay. We have been trying to manage our society somewhat in the way John Lennon of the Beatles says he writes music. "I was just sitting, trying to think of a song," John explained to a reporter, "and I thought of myself sitting there, doing nothing and going nowhere. Once I'd thought of that it was easy to write 'Nowhere Man.'"

The theme "Nowhere Man"—"going nowhere and doing nothing"—is characteristic of an era that has forgotten the "thunders of Sinai." Our great expectations have turned into great disillusionment. Of course, if our disenchantment reminds us to seek wiser guidance than we have found thus far and virtue for the road ahead, we may yet find our way to a better future.

The Value Crisis

It is apparent that there is a value crisis in American culture. We seem to be wandering in an ethical wasteland, with yesterday's convictions mildewed. Robert F. Goheen, president of Princeton University, not an alarmist by nature, voiced his fear that the country is "drifting into a state of general sleaziness of morality and esthetic taste that can destroy not only the quality of life in America but our very system of government."

The facade of an ordered society remains, but, on examination, it has the characteristics of T. S. Eliot's "hollow men," who are its uncertain foundation. Violence, drugs, uninhibited sex, and despair are the ingredients of national disintegration. They testify to the hollowness of men and women devoid of inner resources of mind and spirit.

A nation is no stronger than the moral fiber of its people. Our freedom hinges on the ethical integrity of men and women whose inner convictions issue in dependable and trustworthy character; whose value system enables them to judge what is good and fair, honorable and just; and who dare to stand against the tides that swirl around them.

Rowland R. Hegstad noted recently that when John W. Gardner urged a student audience in Washington, D.C., to restore values to our society, he was asked by a student, "Sir, upon what do you base your values?" After a moment's hesitation, Gardner replied, "I do not know."

If we have no basis for judging what is good and fair, just and honorable, the question, when we wish to be other than honorable and just, is: Why not? What valid reason is there for not doing as I please, however dishonorable, if there is no basis for choosing

47

between right and wrong? If there are no basic guidelines for ethical decision making, what difference does it make what I do?

It may seem trite to suggest that the Ten Commandments are not altogether out of date. They still remain valid, not primarily because Moses said they came from God. They are wise guidelines for human behavior because they grew out of centuries of human trial and error. They are valid because they are basic to the business of living together in society. Just as Sir Isaac Newton's law of gravity revealed something about the material structure of the universe, the Ten Commandments say something about the spiritual structure of the universe.

Suggestively, the social scientists today are saying that, in every culture of the past, something akin to respect for individual human personality has been a guiding principle for ethics. So Albert Schweitzer understood in his insistence on "reverence for life" as an ultimate guideline for ethical behavior. Emil Brunner sounded the same note in his cry for "other-concern."

These ultimate ideals for moral action come home in the Ten Commandments. If I reverence my neighbor, I will not steal from him, neither will I seduce his wife. If I have deep other-concern, I will not cheat my neighbor or bear false witness against him. In the New Testament, love is the ultimate value, and love results in other-concern and in reverence for life that lead me to honor my neighbor and do to him as I would be done by.

The ancient Psalmist asked an unsettling question when his nation was in the process of disintegration: "When the foundations are undermined, what can the good man do?" The most decisive answer to that question is, Start where you are. Renew your loyalty to the abiding values that have their anchors in the structures of God's universe. Spend your life in the service of what is good and fair, honorable and just.

It is later than you think!

Borrowed Name

With a surname borrowed from the man who owned him, George Washington Carver honored the name and inspired his race with hope. He began life as a slave and became an honored scientist and educator.

George was born of slave parents on a farm near Diamond Grove, Missouri. He never knew his birth date, but the year probably was 1860, a time of trouble between Kansas and Missouri over the slavery issue. One moonless night, when George still was a baby, a band of raiders kidnapped him and his mother, Mary. Seeing a chance to make a profit, the abductors offered to return George and his mother to the Carvers in exchange for a horse and money. The Carvers agreed. Unfortunately, after the horse was delivered, the raiders made off with Mary and returned George, somewhat worse for his experience but still alive. George never knew what happened to his mother.

Moses Carver and his wife, Susan, raised George; they taught him to read and write and encouraged his education. George was capable and eager to learn. By the time he was ten years old, he had a remarkable gift for making things grow—a green thumb, everyone said. Hermann Jaegar, a neighbor and a grape grower, took a liking to George and gave him a Bible and other books and encouraged him to work in the vineyards.

After the Civil War, George took off to the West determined to enter college. Rebuffed once because he was a Negro, he made his way to Ames, Iowa, where he entered Iowa College of Agriculture and Mechanic Arts. There he proved to be a genius in botany and agricultural chemistry. Upon graduation, he was invited to remain at Iowa College as a professor.

49

Having proved his worth at his alma mater, the young man was invited by Dr. Booker T. Washington, president of Tuskegee Institute, to become director of agricultural research at the Alabama school. Carver held the post from 1896 until his death in 1943. President Jimmy Carter should be grateful to George Washington Carver for making the lowly peanut respectable, producing more than three hundred items, ranging from soap to candy, from peanuts.

The once-nameless slave did not stop with peanuts. A believer in hard work, initiative, and fidelity to excellence, he made synthetic marble from wood shavings; dyes from clay; and more than one hundred products, including starch, paste, dyes, and candy, from sweet potatoes.

It is significant to remember, too, that Carver did what he did with little more than a makeshift laboratory at Tuskegee. "There's no use to whine, 'Oh, if I only had so-and-so,'" he used to tell his students. "Do it anyhow; use what you find about you." Then he would go with them to junk heaps for bottles, jars, and wire to make what he could not afford to buy. "Equipment is not all in the laboratory," he observed, "but partly in the head of the man running it."

No one would have guessed that the seeds of genius were in George Washington Carver or that the future would reveal unworked seams of intelligence and competence in those whose ancestors were slaves. Despite discrimination and unbelievable hardship, men and women of Carver's race achieved distinction, assumed national leadership, and revealed spiritual and intellectual power.

Other blacks have made marks in every area of human endeavor. On the road to their achievements, they sang of their hurts: "Nobody knows de trouble I'se seen." It was so, and yet they moved ahead. Marian Anderson and Paul Robeson lifted their voices in operatic song and won the plaudits of critics. Jackie Robinson broke the barriers that had made baseball a white preserve and proved his worth as a man and a baseball star. Hank Aaron carried on Robinson's high standards.

Black stars in football, baseball, basketball, and track have dispelled the myth of inferiority. Richard Wright and Alex Haley invaded the world of literature. Martin Luther King, Jr., touched the conscience of the nation when his voice rang in stirring cadence, "I have a dream," a dream of brotherhood and justice in this land of the free.

George Washington Carver believed that hard work, initiative, and fidelity to excellence could lead his people out of their bondage to white prejudice and into the mainstream of society. His achievements, and those of his successors, have proved him right.

Thanks Be to God

Enter his gates with thanksgiving,
    and his courts with praise!
Give thanks to him, bless his name!
For the Lord is good;
    his steadfast love endures forever,
    and his faithfulness to all generations.

Psalm 100, verses 4–5

Thanksgiving Saga

On September 16, 1620, more than 350 years ago, the Pilgrims left Plymouth, England, in the *Mayflower* bound for the New World. In the words of William Bradford, who wrote the narrative of their journey and later became the governor of the colony, "So they committed themselves to the will of God and resolved to proceed."

Some of the Pilgrims had to be left behind because one of their ships sprung a leak, but the remainder "committed themselves to the will of God" and set sail for the New World. They did not guess what suffering they would endure, what agony they would know, before the winter turned to spring. They knew their lot would be a difficult one, more than a little hazardous, but they embarked with faith and hope. They were mindful as they began their venture of the sustaining grace of God they had found in the face of persecution and loss before they left the shelter of the White Cliffs of Dover.

The celebrating of the first Thanksgiving Day after a grim winter in the New World suggests the spirit undergirding the venture of the Pilgrims. They were thankful men and women who knew themselves to be dependent on the grace of God. Having "committed themselves to the will of God," they were resolved to make the best of their situation. So, with incredible fortitude they hung on through the months and years to lay foundations for the nation we love, enriching our national character through the legacy of their perseverance and faith.

The Pilgrims seemed aware that only the thankful man knows himself for what he is, namely, a dependent creature. Edwin

Arlington Robinson voiced an unchanging truth when he wrote in "King Jasper":

> I don't say what God is, but it's a name
> That somehow answers us when we are driven
> To feel and think how little we have to do
> With what we are.

Every faculty we possess, the power to think, to will, and to create, is given to us by a Wise Providence whose ways are past finding out. We speak "with the tongues of men and angels" or in halting ways express our feelings by the courtesy of God. Our capacities for affection and friendship are God's gifts.

The thankful man sees deeper than the man who walks with unfettered pride in his own achievements. He understands that God works in and through the common life of men and touches each with gifts from all. We are, as Paul, the apostle, said, debtors to "a vast cloud of witnesses" whose lives and thoughts have shaped our culture and ourselves. God's benefits are mediated through the hands and minds of both the living and the dead.

Looking back over his long and useful life, Reinhold Niebuhr commented that he could not catalog all the influences that had touched his life. He could not measure the gifts he had received from his family and his friends, his ancestors, and his teachers. They all had influenced him in a hundred ways to shape his thought and his life. His inheritance, he said, gave him "an understanding of religious faith as trust in the meaning of human existence." A "vast cloud of witnesses" ministered to his creative life. He knew he was dependent on many influences and that a gentle conspiracy of nature and of God had nourished his mind and spirit.

If we look into our own experiences, we will see how much we have been blessed by gifts we did not earn. We did not earn the endowments of our minds, the power to perceive the truth, or to walk with wisdom through the days. We did not earn the faith we share. As William Cowper wrote of nature in "The Task":

> Beneath the open sky she spreads the feast,
> 'Tis free to all—'tis every day renewed.

Deep gratitude leads us to cherish the institutions, the memories, and the values that have undergirded our culture. It leads to sharing, to discipline, and to self-giving. The Pilgrims made their response of gratitude in their zeal to share their faith in God. As one of them put it, they could be "stepping stones unto others." And heaven only knows how many have been inspired and blessed by the courage, the faith, and the rigorous discipline of those who gave us our Thanksgiving Day. They taught us the meaning of gratitude and gave us more than a hint of the power of faith to see men and women through the worst and on to triumph, to the glorious light after the storm.

Gifts from the Past

Nobody starts from scratch! All of us stand on the shoulders of others, both living and dead. In the final sentence of *Middlemarch*, George Eliot wrote, "That things are not so ill with you and me as they might have been, is half owing to the number who lived faithfully a hidden life, and rest in unvisited tombs." We can only dimly sense how much we owe to those who rest in "unvisited tombs"—to unsung pioneers and prophets, philosophers and poets, soldiers and saints, who laid foundations for our lives today.

Like Johnny Appleseed planting apple seeds in the hills and valleys of our land, multitudes of men and women who came before us planted knowledge and culture that we have inherited. Our freedom to seek whatever destiny we choose is the bequest of Socrates and Jesus, and of the nobles of Runnymede and the patriots of Valley Forge. We are free because those who lie in "unvisited tombs" lived and died for our freedom. We are debtors to the many who lived faithfully despite "peril, toil, and pain."

In a thousand ways, we reap what we did not plant and inherit what others won for us. If we fly in jet airplanes, it is because the Wright brothers risked their lives to prove the possibility of flying. If we are linked to the wide world by telephone, it is because Alexander Graham Bell risked the scorn of his contemporaries and proved the transmission of the human voice by wire was feasible. A hundred thousand gadgets make life comfortable for us because others toiled, and we have inherited the fruit of their labors.

One of the most powerful motives for achievement is the awareness that we are debtors to those who occupy "unvisited tombs." When we know how much our inheritance cost those who left it to us, we are challenged to contribute what we are able to those who will come after us. A kindly naturalist once impressed a motto on my mind, and it has stayed with me through the years: "Leave the trail better than you found it."

That advice, born in the woods, is appropriate for all of life. If others improved the trails we walk today, leaving cement walks and broad highways, fruited plains and gleaming cities, we can do no less than toil to leave a better world for those who follow us. We would be devoid of the grace of gratitude if we were simply to enjoy our inheritance without seeking to pass it on enriched for generations yet to come.

Auguste Comte was so impressed by the legacy of past ages that he spent his life seeking to enrich the world for the future. The more he studied the past, the more he was impressed by the strivings of his forgotten ancestors and the more he was aware of the debt he ought to pay by way of contributions to his generation. Sir Isaac Newton, knowing how much he had learned from yesterday, insisted that, if he had seen farther than other men, it was because he had stood "on the shoulders of giants." He, in turn, became a giant on whose shoulders other scientists stood in the years ahead.

The past is part of each of us. We cannot turn on a light switch, look at a clock, pound a typewriter, drive an automobile, read a book, put on a pair of shoes, or turn on the television without being a debtor to those who now occupy "unvisited tombs." What is more, our intellectual attainments and our spiritual insights are largely gifts from the past. We are what we are because the blood of our ancestors runs in our veins, and the world they shaped has fashioned us. We cannot escape yesterday.

Only the man who does not know history can be unmoved by the rich gifts that have come to him from the past. One who is aware of the significance of the toilers who preceded him cannot avoid the conclusion that he is called to contribute something to the world that is to be.

Antiques in Perspective

Antique shows continue to intrigue me, even though the quality of the things offered seems to have deteriorated over the years. Pots and pans, old furniture and clocks, tools and half-forgotten gadgets, glassware and dishes, all are available at inflated prices. Things from the past that our ancestors discarded for the new are treasures the present generation seeks with enthusiasm, treasures whose age only makes them more intriguing.

An eighteenth-century chest from somewhere in Connecticut seemed an appropriate reminder that the past still is present. It may be that our interest in antiques suggests a nostalgia for a time when life was easier and less complicated, simpler and with sounder values—a naive wish to recover something dependable and solid from "the good old days."

It would be pleasant to know something of the history of the well-preserved antique chest. Having survived 200 years of good times and bad, wars and rumors of wars, prosperity and depression, and the fortunes of its various owners, it would know something of the achievements and the misfortunes of two centuries of life. I wished the old chest could speak and share some insight and wisdom.

As I thought about the antique chest and other things from the past, I thought of Jeremiah, the prophet. He lived a long life through perilous and difficult times, through forty years of tension, culminating in the destruction of Jerusalem in 586 B.C. He knew the meaning of disaster and loss, but he was aware of the things that endure despite the worst that can happen to a people. He was in touch with the wisdom of his faith.

All through the years preceding the fall of Jerusalem, Jeremiah kept talking about the indestructible antiques of his Hebrew heritage. He warned his people over and over again that their security was insecure without fidelity to the abiding values of justice and truth. He told them that sacrifices were no substitute for spiritual obedience.

In the midst of prosperity, the people of Jerusalem had no time for Jeremiah. Nobody else saw the peril the prophet saw. Assyria had fallen, defeated by the emerging power of Babylon. Why worry about Babylon? After all, things were going well in Judah. The price of grain was high. Values were inflated, but there was plenty of money, at least among the upper classes. Of course, there was cheating and corruption, and religion was a hollow affair of sacrifices without devotion. Why wouldn't Jeremiah just go home and keep still?

But the prophet wouldn't go home and keep still. He went on puncturing the pretensions of the mighty and challenging the deceptions of the politicians. He was upset by the moral rebellion of the people. "You are riding for a fall," he told his annoyed listeners. "God won't stand for your corrupt ways." Then, with thunder in his voice, he said, "Thus says the Lord, 'Stand by the roads and look, and ask for the ancient paths, where the good way is; and walk in it, and find rest for your souls.'"

Quite possibly, we need a modern Jeremiah to remind us of the timeless antiques of human experience. We live too much in time and too little in the timeless. We forget the life of the spirit while we pursue the illusory satisfactions of the world. It was so with Pontius Pilate, as Anatole France pictured him. The corpulent procurator of Judea encountered an old friend he had not seen for years. The two exchanged memories of long careers in the imperial service. "What about the Galilean wonder-worker, Jesus of Nazareth," Pilate's old friend inquired, "the one who was crucified for some crime or other?" "Jesus," Pilate murmured in the closing words of the story, "Jesus of Nazareth? I do not remember the name." Pilate's mental block eased his guilt.

We, too, forget the name of Jesus of Nazareth and the way of the cross while we scramble for security on the secular scene. The intangible timeless is buried beneath an avalanche of cultivated wants. Who can remember Jesus amidst the frantic competition of Wall Street? Who can remember the Galilean or his message in the mad struggle for power in Washington, D.C., or New York City or Chicago? But there is an antique name, Jesus of Nazareth, that is timeless in the midst of time, a name to be treasured as a symbol of all the best in our heritage and to be remembered in good times and bad.

Unfinished History

To say that life today is rooted in the past is not to say we cannot move beyond the past. "Man is an unfinished being, always in the state of becoming," Arnold Toynbee noted. Both man and society are in the process of becoming. "Civilization is a movement, and not a condition, a voyage, not a harbor," Toynbee continued. We do not simply take life as it comes. On the contrary, we are forever evaluating, dissimilating, choosing, and transforming the structures of life and society.

The Spanish, according to Americs Castro, historian of his people, became fixed in the traditions and patterns of the past. "The Spaniard," he wrote, "wedded himself to his legendary religious and artistic beliefs, as did no other European people." The people and their leaders were unwilling to change when change became necessary. They wrapped themselves in their outworn traditions and were unable to venture with hope into the twentieth century. The past grew abundant weeds and underbrush that hemmed in the creative and productive spirit. So, the Spaniard found it incredibly difficult to grow beyond his past.

One of the problems of our society today is that, while some would discard the past as useless, there are others who, like the Spaniard, are wedded to their yesterdays. They cannot let their rose-tinted memories go. Leon Uris noted perceptively in *Topaz* that "Nicole always looked upon the past as a treasured memory, forgetting how she hated it while she lived it." So we often are deceived by our flowered memories, forgetting how we hated the living of the days that begot our memories. Yesteryear really was not as perfect as it seems when seen through the haze of distance.

As we grow older, we frequently forget that tomorrow belongs

63

to those who are young today. If we are disturbed by the "now generation," they are disturbed by us. They think we are the "yesterday generation." Both of us are wrong. The "now generation" needs our finest memories, and we need the vision and the hopes of the young. If we are afraid of change, they are eager for change and newness.

It is suggestive to notice, as Robert E. Neil says, that most college undergraduates have less than one full decade of "usable past" at their disposal. They have only fragmentary knowledge of twentieth-century history before their time. The oldest, therefore, have only seven years of memory since they were high school sophomores, a time when current events begin to be seen in focus. "Inevitably, therefore," Neil says, "the post senile generation over 30 [has lived long enough] to see more than one set of national and international issues come and go, [and] is likely to see today's headlines in a longer perspective."

On the other hand, those of us who are middle-aged or older are disposed to be wedded to our traditions, so that we are reluctant to accept changes that seem to threaten our security. We remember the individualism of yesterday, and we resent mass movements. We recall the wide open spaces of the past, and we are disturbed by a population explosion that has made many of our cities a nightmare. Our nostalgia takes us back to a time when discipline and respect for authority were accepted as necessities, and we are upset by contemporary disregard for both discipline and authority.

The mood of the older generation is akin to that expressed in Alfred Lord Tennyson's "Morte d'Arthur" when Sir Bedivere talks with King Arthur after the disintegration of the Round Table:

Ah! my Lord Arthur, whither shall I go?
.   .   .   .

I see the true old times are dead,
When every morning brought a noble chance
And every chance brought out a noble knight.

But the whole Round Table is dissolved,
Which was an image of the mighty world
And I, the last, go forth companionless.

To say the least, we are bewildered because so many are inclined to forget our common heritage. So many seem ungrateful.

Try Gratitude

It was customary in my boyhood for the family to gather around the piano on Sunday evenings to sing hymns. My grandmother managed the keyboard while mother sang alto, father tenor, and my sister and I carried the tune. One of my father's favorite hymns was

> Count your blessings, name them one by one;
> Count your many blessings, see what God hath done.

There were times when the blessings seemed a little skimpy and the problems sizable, but the hymn gave a lift to our spirits.

Counting blessings was something of a chore for a ten-year-old boy, somewhat subdued by the affluence of a neighborhood friend who seemed to have everything from an electric train to a new bicycle. I had plenty to eat, a roof over my head, and a battered bicycle with a tire that persistently went flat. Then, too, our next-door neighbor was a problem. After some months, she still refused to return my errant baseball, which had landed in her garden one sunny afternoon. It seemed to me that the neighbor was a distinctly negative blessing.

In retrospect, it is clear that I was extremely fortunate as a youngster. There were innumerable, intangible blessings that had not occurred to me. I hadn't thought to count them. Then, too, I was inclined to accentuate the negative in my situation, such as having to do daily chores and practicing for my piano lessons.

Most of us, I suspect, overlook many of our blessings, especially when we are beset by hard times. We forget that, as W. Mathews noted, "it is not helps, but obstacles; not facilities, but difficulties, that make men." We prefer helps and facilities and feel put upon when we meet obstacles and difficulties. Nevertheless, even our problems have possibilities hidden beneath the surface.

When we are honest with ourselves, it is clear that our blessings outweigh the negatives in our experience, if we are perceptive enough to include the intangibles. There are the warmth of friendship, the deeps of affection, the splendor of loyalty, and the strength of faith. These have no price tag, but they are meaningful beyond measure. When Shakespeare viewed the intangibles that touched his life, he wrote, "O Lord, who lends me life, lend me a heart replete with thankfulness."

While a small boy may not be able to appreciate the intangibles that inspire gratitude, we adults are, or should be, more discriminating. Walt Whitman noted that the hinge in your little finger "puts all machinery to shame." What is more, our capacity to think—to reason from a premise to a conclusion—is a gift more precious than all the gold of Midas. Who can measure the worth of memory that enables us to travel back along the roads we have wandered in years gone by?

We did not win our heritage of freedom to speak and write as we please. It is a gift of those who strove for it in "peril, toil, and pain." It is ours to cherish and keep for the generations yet unborn. The "purple mountain majesties" that rise "above the fruited plain" are ours to enjoy through the courtesy of God.

There is that strange, sweet mystery of love that binds us together in families and the brooding devotion that keeps us loyal to one another in times of stress. There are possibilities of mind and spirit that lurk in our children, waiting only to be awakened by some surprising challenge. Conscience is alive in us, prodding us to pursue the right when the allure of the wrong is strong. Vital powers in us await only the emergence of motives strong enough to elicit them.

Beauty lies in wait around us, and we have eyes with which to see. Even the drabbest scenery becomes a fairyland beneath a canopy of snow. The romance of the spring is one to mock the mightiest of man-made dramas. The turning of the leaves to gold, red, and yellow when the summer's end has come yields a pageant whose garmenture is beyond our dreaming.

A lad of ten would not count such blessings, but we who have come to maturity should find them worthy to be measured against the strains of our days.

Routine Passage

So far as the ancient Jews were concerned, Samaria was an unpleasant place. It wasn't the countryside that was disagreeable. The landscape was by no means unattractive. The valleys were lovely, and there were refreshing wells along the way. The trouble was the people. They had some Jewish blood in them, but they were like relatives you would like to forget. Their religion was distasteful to the Jews, and they were not inclined to be either pleasant or thoughtful to them as they passed through Samaria.

Unfortunately for the Sons of Abraham, Samaria lay between Judea and Galilee, and if someone wanted to get from one place to the other, there was Samaria in between. As John said of Jesus, "He had to pass through Samaria." It was routine, necessary, and inevitable, but it wasn't pleasant.

It should be said that Samaria always lies between Galilee and Judea, that is, between where we are and where we wish to go. There isn't any easy route from where we stand today to where we would like to be tomorrow. Samaria inevitably lies along the itinerary. We just can't avoid the disagreeable routine, no matter where we are headed. Every achievement is nine-tenths drudgery, nine-tenths plodding through Samaria, wishing we were in Jerusalem. It's futile to dream of shortcuts.

Most youngsters seem to think the grind of going to school is mostly a matter of passing through Samaria. This is especially true in springtime. School gets to be dull routine, the same old road to the same place every morning. Day after day there are the same teachers in the same rooms pouring on the inevitable assignments. If there is any Jerusalem in the distance, it seems too far removed to make much difference.

No matter who you are, you have to grapple with a lot of dullness and sweat through the disagreeable along the road to where you are going. Of course, nobody outside sees the dullness, the wearisome routine. That is why it is so dull. Nobody other than William Makepeace Thackeray understood the drudgery of twenty years of struggle that lay behind his *Vanity Fair*. Everybody saw the finished product and acclaimed it, but nobody knew the years of Samaria that lay behind Thackeray's Jerusalem. But, like Jesus, Thackeray "had to pass through Samaria."

Since we are compelled to spend so much time in Samaria, we may as well get used to it. Some people are miserable because they resent the drudgery of Samaria. The years seem dull. The endless sameness of things is more than they can endure. Sometimes they take to drugs or drink to relieve the monotony. They run to this nightclub or that or join the swingers, hoping that possibly they can escape from Samaria, even if they don't get to Jerusalem.

It is easy to miss the possibilities in the routine passages of life, and, yet, even Samaria need not be all dullness. There is such a thing as finding a glow in the plodding routine of life. One thoughtful woman put the truth delightfully when she was asked, "How are things going for you?" She replied, "Oh, I'm just coasting along in a happy rut." And that, I suspect, is life's task: to make your rut a happy one. It may be rugged, and sometimes deep, but it need not be miserable.

Making your rut a happy one hinges on knowledge wrought in faith that the ground on which you stand is "holy ground," whether it be in Samaria or in Jerusalem. We need to know that God is just as close to Samaria as He is to Jerusalem and that He breaks through more often in the ordinary than in great moments of achievement or arrival. When we stop to think, it is strange to discover that God usually breaks through when we are bogged down in Samaria. That is where most of the really important things happen to us, back in the shadows where nobody else can see. We need God most in the days of drudgery, when there isn't much to lift our spirits. When we give Him a chance, He makes us see that doing common tasks is part of His will for us. In Samaria, God fashions our souls for seeing and understanding. Necessarily, you and I have to "pass through Samaria."

Values Worth Keeping

In his story "Babylon Revisited," F. Scott Fitzgerald pictured a man in a Paris bar after the Wall Street debacle of 1929. The bartender asked the troubled man, "Did you lose a lot in the crash?" The answer came, "I lost everything I really wanted in the boom."

In retrospect, it is clear that we lost much that we really wanted during the affluence of our recent history. During the epoch of "conspicuous consumption," our lives were sustained by the things we were able to accumulate and consume. These, in effect, became outward props for both our egos and our security. We wanted the things that money could buy but overlooked the things money could not buy.

Because it is easier to be permissive on a fat budget than on a slim one, we assumed the recording angel had gone on a protracted vacation. The old virtues we once cherished became optional—matters of convenience to be abandoned if inconvenient. We got ahead by going along, as if integrity, honor, and virtue were old-fashioned, Victorian ideas.

The "faith of our fathers" seemed a little naive in our time of prosperity, and, for many, it slipped down the drain. The old virtues of integrity and the whole truth became shibboleths of an outmoded, middle-class morality. Swingers had their day. It was a heady time of indifference toward the ethical ideals held sacred by our forefathers.

It may be that in hard times we will regain some of what we lost in affluence. The "faith of our fathers" seems to be "living still" in the obscure corners of our minds and hearts and moving toward center stage, as if, in the midst of anxiety and uncertainty, we are seeking inner props for the outward ones that have been crumbling. Integrity is coming to be the *summum bonum* after a time of permissiveness led us into a period of no-confidence. Even some of the swingers are coming to the conclusion that their life-style is not as fulfilling as they thought.

In 1961, New York was flooded by the rumor that the federal government had taken the motto "In God We Trust" off the lowly one-dollar bill. Hedda Hopper, the Hollywood columnist, was so upset by the rumor, according to Cleveland Amory, that she discussed it with socialite Annie Slater, who said, "What have they got in mind as a replacement?"

We don't seem to have found any adequate replacement for God in our life, at least not if we expect our age of no-confidence to become a time of confidence again. When David saw "violence and strife in the city," he called on the Lord. There are many now who seem to be approaching the wisdom of David. At least the popularity of prayer groups for government officials in Washington lends credence to that assumption.

If we are coming to understand that faith in God, nourished by prayer and worship, undergirds the integrity we so urgently need in our society, we may begin to recover some of the things we lost in our permissive affluence. There is an intimate relationship between faith and works, if faith becomes for us "the assurance of things hoped for, the conviction of things not seen."

The glue that holds our free society together is trust—confidence that those who sell will not cheat those who buy, and vice versa; assurance that those who represent us in government can't be bought; trust that lawyers and judges will be honest in seeking justice; and faith that husbands will be loyal to their wives and wives to their husbands.

If the motto "In God We Trust" is a statement of fact and not merely a pious hope, we will recover in these difficult times what we lost in our affluent prosperity.

Things Are Not All Black

Mark Twain once wrote a story that he called "The Terrible Catastrophe." In the course of the story, he got his characters into such a fix that, whatever any one of them did, they all would be destroyed. As the great humorist considered the impasse at which he had arrived, he felt that the situation for his characters was hopeless. Therefore, he concluded the story by saying: "I have these characters in such a fix that I cannot get them out. Anyone who thinks he can is welcome to try."

The world today is in a fix, and a lot of individuals likewise are snarled in one predicament or another. We may be disposed to throw up our hands and say, "Anybody who thinks he can unravel the plot and make something of it is welcome to try." No matter which way we turn, the plot thickens, and things look worse instead of better.

Commonly, we are inclined to accentuate all the negatives when things look black. But, in every situation, there are positives that need to be recognized. So a British prime minister understood when he received a diplomatic envoy from Central Europe. The envoy told a story of suspicion, intrigue, hatred, and unrest. Silence fell between the two men when the report was concluded. Then, abruptly, the prime minister pushed toward the diplomat a bowl of roses, as if seeing in their beauty some token of present hope. "Bury your face in all that loveliness," he said simply, "and thank God."

It is true enough that our world is in trouble, but plenty of good things are still left—roses and stars and sunsets. There are homes radiant with love and trust and men and women of integrity and honor, illumining the business streets of the nation.

71

There are young men and women who continue to dream dreams and see visions of what can be. There are builders, men who believe in the future and prove it by taking calculated risks to implement their faith.

Even behind the Iron Curtain, there are evidences that positive factors are at work. There are those who go on protesting in the name of human rights. What is more, the church in the Soviet bloc is Communism's headache and freedom's great hope.

The world was in a frightful fix that day on the beaches of Dunkirk, with Hitler riding high and the British army at bay with its back to the sea. But there was the positive devotion and courage of a nondescript collection of men and women who manned a thousand little boats. Some of them never had been to sea before, but when a leader's voice asked, "Will ye fetch the lads back?" they went out and they brought the lads back.

Usually, it is the intangibles of faith, courage, and tenacity that are the decisive positives in the middle of negatives that seem so apparent. Tides turn and plots begin to unravel when we get over the notion that things are so bad they can't be made better. When we begin with real faith to search out the good things—the values that last, no matter what comes—we can find ways to deal with the worst and make something of it.

Mebane Ramsey paints a word picture that strikes to the heart of our need as we venture into our tomorrows. She describes a group of visitors going through the Carlsbad caverns in New Mexico. An eleven-year-old boy and his seven-year-old sister were among those surveying the wonders of the underground caves. When they came to the deepest point in the caverns, the lights went out, and the little girl began to cry. The boy comforted his sister, "Don't you cry. There's a man here who knows how to turn the lights on."

When life's plot seems "black as the pit from pole to pole," God still can turn the lights on. As an ancient seer wrote, "The light shines in darkness, and the darkness cannot put it out."

Seasonal Pageantry

The sky is low, the clouds are mean,
A travelling flake of snow
Across a barn or through a rut
Debates if it will go.

A narrow wind complains all day
How some one treated him;
Nature, like us, is sometimes caught
Without her diadem.

"Beclouded" by EMILY DICKINSON

Winter Snow

There is a snow rabbit leaning against a light post and icicles hanging from the church roof across the street. The children have made a snowman in the park I can see from my window as I write, and the world dances and sparkles in its mantle of white. It is cold outside and passersby are bundled and muffled as befits the chill of the air.

Snow changes the contours of everything, rounding rough corners and blunting sharp edges. The garbage can isn't a garbage can anymore. It is a little old man, squat and fat, hunched against the wind and wearing a white stocking cap. The trees are etched in white, and the bushes bend low beneath their weight of snow. A clump of weeds has humps like pussy willows done in white.

A little Volkswagen, nearly buried by a blanket of snow, looks like an igloo with a touch of black protruding. It will be stuck where it is for a while. The church steps have lost their character and turned into what appears to be a slide for the children. Walks haven't been shoveled and footprints stand out, as Walter de la Mare noted in "Winter":

> Oh, I remember now
> A dell of snow,
> Frost on the bough;
> None there but I:
> Snow, snow, and a wintry sky.
>
> None there but I,
> And footprints one by one,
> Zigzaggedly,
> Where I had run.

75

The sky is wintry with ominous clouds, dark and brooding in the west, perhaps foretelling more snow to come. Planes are circling above, stacked up and filled with travelers hoping to land. Autos are slipping and sliding on the icy streets, and only the brave dare the cold. The walking is treacherous, inviting a fall.

The broad expanse of the earth, covered with a white blanket, is both forbidding and beautiful. Boris Pasternak said it well when he wrote: "The snow smoothed and rounded all contours. It could not quite conceal the winding bed of a stream which in the spring would rush down to the viaduct below the railway bank but at present was tucked up in the snow like a child in a cot with its head under the eiderdown."

Jack Frost has painted the windowpanes with myriad shapes, sometimes like mountains, with their peaks looming high against the white outside. He has sketched an Indian chief, all decked in feathers, on my study window. I hope the Indian will stay awhile and not melt away too soon. Indian chiefs don't come for visits too often these days.

The winter wind seems to be in a hurry, adding to the chill, as if to say, "I'm in tune with the times." Even the bare branches of the trees shiver and rattle and shake themselves free of snow. The wind seems to snarl at times like an angry dog scaring strangers away. It is no wonder we hurry home from our toil and slide in from the cold with sighs of relief.

The snow doesn't seem to mind if the wind whips it into drifts, blocking highways and city streets and making a shambles of traffic. It seems to know it can't stay for long, so it may as well make the most of its chance to make itself felt. I suppose it would rather be white than slush, with its beauty and wildness gone.

Even the winter moon seems cold when it peeks through the clouds. It invites the howling of wolves in the wilderness and sends wild creatures into their burrows for security. It evokes the delight of young and old who see it in all its glory through windowpanes. But it is a forbidding moon in the cold of the night.

If we have not lost our zest for life, there is charm and loveliness in our winter wonderland. It stirs the imagination and delights the spirit. It is the prophecy of the earth's rebirth in the spring nourishing the greening to come.

Christmas Murmurs and Fragments

Times were discouraging and difficult when "the morning stars sang together," heralding the first Christmas. The hard fist of Rome was evident in the census, calling for the registration of citizens of the empire. Joseph and Mary, caught up in the census, traveled to Bethlehem to enroll their names on Caesar Augustus' tax list, even though Mary was about to give birth to her child.

Bethlehem was not an attractive place, packed full of nomads who came regularly to the little town to buy grain and to sell their woven cloth and their cheeses, as they still do today. There were, in addition, all those who had come to Bethlehem for the census. The noisy, smelly crowd, braying donkeys, and tethered camels contributed to the din of the marketplace. Hints of poverty and hardship were easy to recognize.

The shepherds who frequented Bethlehem were a motley lot, submerged in the struggle to live. Life was not easy for them in the fields where they watched their flocks. The heat of the summer was stifling, no less difficult to endure than the bitter chill of the winter. Times, for them, always were hard and Bethlehem provided little in the way of respite.

Bethlehem, when Joseph and Mary arrived, suggested nothing in the way of good news. The flea-bitten inn was full and would not have been a fit place for the birth of a child even at best. Since the "days were accomplished that she should be delivered," Joseph installed his wife in a cave such as was used, and still is used, to shelter sheep and cattle from the cold and rain. "And she gave birth to her first-born son, and wrapped him in swaddling cloths, and laid him in a manger."

77

It would seem that God should have been able to find a more fitting place for the birth of an important personage, and a better time, too. A palace would have been more appropriate, except for the fact that most people are not born in palaces, and God had common people in mind when He selected a manger for the birthplace of Jesus. Then, too, since hard times are normal for most people most of the time, He planned the birth of the Master in just such a time.

Possibly our experience of life's hardness is not so poignant as it was for those who shared the streets of Bethlehem, yet I dare say it is enough for our taste. The world still is a rather ghastly, unpromising place at times. Poverty and hunger still stalk the streets of every nation on earth. Tyranny, as brutal as Rome's, claims its victims in half the world. Corruption mocks the ethic of Bethlehem's star.

Life does not change very much even though we change the geography and the century. We are kin to those on the teeming streets of Bethlehem and they to us. We go on and on, trying to make sense of life's struggle and to find some meaning in it, some reason to hope. We really should not expect that a star would appear over Bethlehem, or Chicago either, for that matter.

Curiously, though, a "Silent Night, Holy Night," came to Bethlehem, to shepherds and wise men, to those sensitive enough to catch its meaning. It comes to us, too, but often, as Edwin Arlington Robinson wrote in "Captain Craig," we do not listen:

> ...we know the truth has been
> Told over to the world a thousand times;—
> But we have had no ears to listen yet
> For more than fragments of it; we have heard
> A murmur now and then, an echo here
> And there, . . .

But our days are so burdened with a number of things that the murmurs are muted, and we catch only fragments of the good news the wise men and the shepherds heard.

We can't seem to understand the truth, "told over to the world a thousand times," that God can pick us up and lift us out of our despondency, our desperation, and our fears and keep us steady with hope and trust. It isn't that the world changes overnight, but

78

rather that our perspective changes. Our mood is infused with a steady trust that the love of God will see us through whatever harsh circumstances we face. Though

> ... hate is strong
> And mocks the song
> Of peace on earth, good-will to men,

still "God is our ruler yet." He is not mocked by the stupidities and follies of men and women. He

> ... is not dead; nor doth he sleep!

Travel to Rome if you will. The Forum, the Colosseum, the Circus, the crumbling walls, and the imperial roads are but relics of a grandeur that is gone. But Rome is vibrantly alive with evidence of the enduring power of Bethlehem's child. The kneeling multitudes in a million churches throughout the world testify to the continuing authority of the living Christ. The bells that peal on Christmas day with joy and hope mock the empty and shattered walls of fallen empires.

However muted by the tumult and shouting of men and nations, the murmurs of Bethlehem's message still pervade the Christmas season. Feelings of affection and generous love invade the homes we share. Goodwill infects our human relationships, almost in spite of ourselves. Busy though we may be, we cannot altogether escape the impact of Eternal Love transcending the possible.

That first Christmas night, the shepherds, burdened by problems, fears, and misgivings about life itself, were suddenly aware they could trust the love of God. He had not left them alone to make the best of a bad situation. He is the Living Comrade of life who cared enough to seek them out in the darkness of the night, even though they were unimportant people in an unimportant province of the Roman Empire. In one flashing moment of insight, they knew God had invaded their lives with love that could be trusted, and, henceforth, life never would be the same again.

Life never will be the same for us either if the truth, "told over to the world a thousand times," finds a sure anchor in our minds and hearts.

Spring Miracles

The miraculous surrounds us in the spring. It didn't seem possible in January that the seemingly dead earth would come to flower in May. Barren trees, arching their branches toward the sky only yesterday, are green with buds and leaves. The marsh snow has melted; frogs are croaking; and crickets are singing again. The lilac bushes, whose tips seemed brown and worn, have come alive with the promise of beauty.

The dogwood that defied the winter, while clinging in quiet desperation to the nourishing earth, is alive with white bloom and flourishing leaves. Tulips, whose bulbs escaped the hunger of prying squirrels in their winter search for food, are rioting with color. Who would have guessed the latent glory of mere bulbs? The pussy willows, only dry sticks a little while ago, are furry things of grace and beauty.

Grass is green again, marked only here and there by the burns of winter's ice and snow. My neighbor has been working in his yard, cutting and trimming his lawn. He is grateful for the chance to dig in the earth of his garden of flowers and to encourage the green carpeting of his lawn. He has a green thumb, and the neighbors are beneficiaries of his patient labors. His yard is trim and lovely, a joy to behold.

The cardinals seem happier. They appeared forlorn, their red coats etched against the snow of winter, but now they are singing, building their nests, and mating. Some time ago, the robins came back to join them after a summer siesta in the South away from the snow and the ice. Song sparrows, like the robins, have made their long trek to the North to mate, nest, and rear their families.

When I watched a robin pecking for worms, I wondered what

had happened to the worms when snow and ice covered the ground. Did they freeze, then come to life, or perhaps hibernate like bears? Maybe some "worm expert" can enlighten me! The worms seem quite well, judging by the seeming delight of the hungry robin digging for them across the street from my window.

The pageantry of the seasons mocks the garmenture of kings, and May affirms the glory of God. After the long winter, the earth is bursting with life and beauty. William Cowper celebrated spring's abundance in "The Task":

> Beneath the open sky she spreads the feast;
> 'Tis free to all—'tis every day renewed;
> Who scorns it starves deservedly at home.

If we miss the tendrils of the climbing ivy, the fresh leaves of maple and elm trees, crocuses and tulips, and singing birds and dancing butterflies, we starve ourselves.

May, of course, brings with it the promise of summer, the cookouts and the picnics, days of vacation, boating on the lakes, or climbing in the mountains. It is a time of anticipation and joy. Before long, we will load the family car and be off with fishing rods and gear to our favorite haunts. We can forget the winter's toil and look forward to days in the sun.

It is not really strange, I suppose, that when the earth comes to life in the spring, we do, too. Our own rejuvenation is part of the miracle of springtime. Pessimism and discouragement turn into optimism and hope. Something about the aliveness of the earth communicates itself to the human spirit and rubs itself into our bones. We cannot escape the newness of life around us. It calls to the newness and undiscourageable hope in us.

It may be that the coming of spring is God's way of reminding us that there always is a time for beginning again. No matter how dark and foreboding the winter or how burdensome the toils we have known, a time of renewal will come. Old things pass away, and the new and the fresh arrive. The hurts and the failures of yesterday find an anodyne in the spring, and, with courage and hope, we make new beginnings.

April Resurrection

The cold and snow of February are memories now, fading into the mists of memory as spring comes on. Tender roots, not long since locked in the frozen earth, have come alive to suck new strength from the soil. The barren trees of winter reveal the miracle of new birth, with hints of green promising full leaves to come. Gentle rains have washed the land and fed reviving brooks.

We have packed our skis, skates, and winter boots and have sent overcoats, along with heavy suits, to the cleaners to await the coming of another winter. We know it will come, just as we knew in January and February that April showers and flowers would come. We know because we are familiar with the wondrous pageantry of the seasons. As Vachel Lindsay wrote of the advent of spring in "Chinese Nightingale":

> One thing I remember:
> Spring came on forever,
> Spring came on forever.

There is a quiet gentleness about April, with soft winds blowing warmth over the once-chilled earth. With the renewed creativity of the earth, tulips, awaiting the time to bloom with beauty, have pushed their tender spikes above the ground. Pussy willows are awakening from their long winter's sleep, and the dogwood has come alive again. My neighbor has been puttering with his power lawn mower. Having been laid up for the winter, the machine has been sputtering, reluctant to resume its spring and summer labors. Another neighbor has been washing his automobile, working as if he relished the chance to be outside and to exercise in manual labor. The boys are playing softball in the park. So, the world this spring, as in innumerable other springs, has come alive again.

82

All in all, we have caught something of the spirit of the season. We are more hopeful now than we were; we are more optimistic about the future. Renewed in mind and heart by the earth's rebirth, we feel more adequate for the challenges we face. The pessimism of the recession is becoming the optimism of recovery. Who can be glum in the midst of the earth's promise? The resurrection mood of Easter infects us all.

Then, too, the robins are back, cocking their heads to listen for wriggling worms beneath the sod, and the cardinals, who stayed to brave the winter's chill, are nesting again. The chickadees have resumed their cheerful hopping from limb to limb, as if to shrug off the memory of snow and cold. Even the pigeons seem happier now, strutting on the reviving grass of parks, where lonely folk scatter food for them.

Members of the Knights of the Flower, a church group, have been hard at work planting flowers, digging in the earth as if they rejoiced to put their hands into the damp earth. Their zinnias, petunias, daisies, and pansies soon will be pushing shoots toward the sky. The churchyard will reflect the ardor of their toil through the days to come, and they will find deep satisfaction in their menial labor.

Pity the man or woman who has no eyes to see, no feeling for the resurrection of spring. Surprisingly, there are some who walk with unseeing eyes and feelings wrapped in the cocoon of their own imagined ills. And if these people meet, as in Henry Kirke White's "Ode to Disappointment":

> A peevish April day,
> A little sun, a little rain,

they complain that all is vain, unmoved by the wonder and the crowning beauty of a world refreshed.

There is no ill so grave as to thwart the spirit's lift if we have eyes to see what God has done and feelings to respond to the resurrection of the earth. The hallelujahs of Easter time are a fit response to the leafy flowering of the spring. The miracle of new life can touch us all and push us with renewed hope to the tasks that command our hands and minds. Sadness should turn to laughter and weariness to zest as we share the wonder of spring.

Easter Renewal

The night before Easter had been a traumatic one for the disciples. Tortured by memories of One they had loved and trusted, they could not sleep. Haunted by despair and self-doubt, they could not see the way ahead. Feelings of guilt were very strong in them. In the Garden of Gethsemane, they had slept when Jesus had asked them to "watch and pray." When their Lord was arrested, they had "all left Him and fled" for their lives.

While the shadows of the night hung over them, it was clear to the disciples that they had been more cowardly than courageous. They were not proud of themselves. They wondered if they had spent three years of their lives for a dream that had died on the cross with their Lord. Obviously, they had not done too well as "fishers of men." Maybe they had best return to their boats and their nets.

The defeatist mood of the disciples was starkly revealed when Mary Magdalene, Joanna, and Mary, the mother of James, reported their experience at the empty tomb. The Resurrection account seemed to the disciples "an idle tale," and they did not believe the women. The drama had been played out on Good Friday, and it was absurd to try to give it a hopeful ending.

But, as Albert Payson Terhune wrote in his last note, "God always finishes His sentences," and the hopeful ending was anything but absurd. Easter dawn was the end of the sentence, and what had seemed to the disciples at first "an idle tale" turned into an invincible reality that galvanized their energies, renewed their hope, and sent them on their way to "upset the world."

The skeptics may scoff at the empty tomb, but the power of the Resurrection to transform men and women from groveling,

84

defeated individuals to men and women of dynamic and purpose is difficult to refute. The cowards of Good Friday became men of courage who stood their ground against those who sought to silence them. They risked martyrdom with cheerful goodwill, remembering the words of Jesus, "In the world you shall have tribulation, but be of good cheer, I have overcome the world."

In many ways, we identify with the disciples after Good Friday. We are inclined to agree with Shakespeare that "the evil that men do lives after them; the good is oft interred with their bones." The good, the true, and the beautiful often seem to be at the mercy of might and power, violence and cruelty. The creative, dynamic power of love, forgiveness, and integrity seems to us an "idle tale" in the world we know.

It is our skepticism that leads to our cowardice. Our unwillingness to be eccentric enough to say no to deceit and lying suggests we doubt the values implicit in the name of Christ. Because we question the Resurrection, we hesitate to stand against the tide of moral decay. Why struggle in a cause that is lost? We may as well "eat, drink, and be merry."

The Resurrection experience for the disciples meant renewal of faith and hope and recovery of resolution to go on in loyalty to the living Christ. Their labors to win the world were not an exercise in futility. On the contrary, they were one with the purposes of God. If, in the providence of God, they had only one day more to live, they still had to live with themselves. So why should they live with their worst selves if they could live instead with better ones and thus leave the world better than they found it?

If Easter means to us what it came to mean to the disciples, it will involve a renewal of faith in the validity of love, truth, integrity, and loyalty to what we know to be right. It will revive our courage to reject the blandishments of deception and dishonesty and send us into the future with quiet trust in what the Apostle Paul called "the more excellent way."

Affairs of Nature

There is a tide in the affairs of nature that inspires birds to mate and to build nests in which to nurture their young. The drama occurs each summer, as we watch from the porch of our summer retreat in the Colorado mountains. In due time, when the valley is in full bloom, the young emerge uncertainly to test their wings, while their seniors watch with anxious concern.

The feisty hummingbirds arrive annually in late May or early June from their winter haven in Mexico. Broad-tailed hummers come first to be followed a little later by ruby-throats and rufous hummers. They are a quarrelsome breed, fighting each other for places on the feeders we provide for them. By mid-August, forty or fifty of them swarm around the feeders, jockeying for position and pushing each other or dive-bombing their fellows as they drink the sugar water.

Rufous hummers are the most aggressive. Even when they are outnumbered, they manage to frighten off their larger cousins with zooming dives, their sharp bills poised to strike. When they have had their fill of sugar water, they perch in a nearby tree ready to threaten ruby-throats and broad-tails daring to feed.

Graceful swallows make their nests in the eaves of the porch. When the young break out of their eggs, they make a frightful racket while their elders fly in and out bearing food to nourish the growth of their offspring. The swift, wheeling flight of the busy parents is a joy to watch as they sweep unerringly to the small opening to the nest, pause briefly, and are off again in singing flight.

The young swallows leave their nest in mid-August, seemingly born to flight. While the young chickadees and nuthatches seem a little bumbling when they try their wings, fluttering in the trees to dry their feathers, the swallows sweep from their nest as if they always had known how to fly.

Year after year, two pairs of tanagers—the males with their red heads, yellow bodies, and black wings, and the females with muted yellow bodies tinged with green—make their nests nearby. They are shy birds, cautiously pausing now and then to drink from the sugar-water cups and then quickly departing to the safety of a treetop. Their young lack the bright coloring typical of the elders, as if time alone could nourish beauty.

A downy woodpecker, his black and white feathers glinting in the sun, is something of a loner. He is a noisy chap, clinging to the bark of an ancient pine tree, cocking his head to listen, and then pecking into the bark to capture elusive bugs. Where his mate hides, or where her nest is hidden, we do not know. He keeps her out of sight while he does the culinary chores.

Four cackling blue jays keep us busy filling grain-packed suet feeders. They are gluttons, clinging precariously to perches designed for chickadees, nuthatches, and grosbeaks and gorging themselves with huge chunks of suet. They seem to resent the intrusion of lesser birds and make their displeasure evident with their loud cackling.

The gentle mourning doves are a joy to watch, feeding quietly on the grain we leave on the ground each day. They walk with stately tread, their brown bodies tinged with white feathers blending into the ground. They are content to share the seed we leave for them with blue jays, chickadees, and finches. We have not found their nests, but, in late August, they bring their brood to share the scattered grain. They have an uncanny way of noticing the neighborhood cat slinking in the bushes and leave their feeding place forthwith.

The pageantry of the summer season is an endless one, repeated year by year. The song of the wren, the cry of the killdeer, the plaintive notes of the mourning dove, and the drumming chant of the woodpecker mingle with the roar of the nearby river. We rejoice in the gentle conspiracy of nature and God revealed in the creative flood tide of the summer.

June Reverie

In the midst of June, there is, as Charles Warner notes, "a good deal of fragmentary conversation going on among the birds." Cardinals and robins seem to be communicating with remarkable facility, enjoying what to us is a mystery. Chickadees, not so long on conversation, hop and flit from branch to branch with an agility their feathered friends cannot match.

Spring put an end to the last clutches of winter and left June free to explode with life. Oaks and elms, rested by their winter hibernation, are in full leaf, offering their generous shade to all who wish relief from the broiling sun. Irises are in bloom and peonies in fat bud. Forget-me-nots have begun their summer stand. Tulips, those early bloomers, are more than a little tired now, their petals beginning to fall.

Out in the countryside, a lazy hawk drifts silently, his keen eyes seeking the movement of an unwary field mouse on land well tilled and planted. The early radishes are ready for the table, and the peas are in bloom. Ere long lettuce and asparagus will be ripe for harvest and our tables will tell us that the June crops are here.

June is a mellow month, with brooks running joyfully, watering the wild flowers along their banks. Samuel Taylor Coleridge captures the spirit of this time in "The Rime of the Ancient Mariner":

> A noise like of a hidden brook
> In the leafy month of June,
> That to the sleeping woods all night
> Singeth a quiet tune.

It is a time to wander in the woods and to feel the wonder of growing things, mocking the genius of humankind to match the creative genius of nature.

It is not surprising that the lure of vacation time is upon us. Even though we have to wait for July or August to get away from it all, we dream in June. We have fondled our fishing tackle, tested leaders, and even practiced casting in the backyard. Our minds turn to the special fishing hole where we missed the big one last summer. Maybe our luck will be better next time out. Before we know it, we will be

> ... knee-deep in June,
> 'Bout the time strawberries melts
> On the vine,

as James Whitcomb Riley wrote in "Knee-Deep in June." Apples will be coming on along with cherries and raspberries, all to be sampled while we cast for bass from a boat or wait for the strike of an unwary trout. Who would have guessed in March that the nobby branches of a pear tree would have turned silvery with leaves and budding fruit?

If we are sensitive, we really wonder "what is so rare as a day in June?" With the lark on the wing and the raccoons on the prowl, there is something seductively beautiful about the resurrection of all life that is unfolding before us. Pheasants are running along the growing corn rows and nesting in the swale. Ducks have settled down to raise their young.

The world seems to shimmer in loveliness in June, and our spirits rise. The dull, dark days of winter are only a memory now as we cook hamburgers on the backyard grill and loll in the sun, hoping for a tan rather than a sunburn. If the water in the lake seems a little chill, the beaches are inviting, and the sand is warm. The grass in the parks is green again, and picnics are in style once more.

There are some, like Helen Hunt Jackson, who prefer "October's bright blue weather" to the "suns and skies and clouds of June," but June is the time I cherish most. The falling leaves of autumn and the riot of color that comes with fall have charm and beauty, but they mark the end, not the beginning, of nature's creativity. June is inviting and joyous; October is the ominous invitation to winter. I prefer the beginning to the end, for in the beginning is the yet-unfolded glory that is to come.

Whichever season we cherish most, we should not quarrel with the economy of God. The pageantry of the seasons is the pageantry of life itself, with times of creation and growth and times of decline and death. Each has its place in the structure of things. There is a time for spring and a time for winter.

Lazy Days

August is a time for sunburn and cookouts, singing crickets and croaking frogs. Trout in my favorite stream are hiding in the deep water, shaded by overhanging bushes. A hoot owl, perched in a tall pine outside my bedroom window, disturbs my sleep at night. The barn swallows have raised their young and departed from their annual nesting place in the eaves of my front porch.

Down in the swamp by the river, a mallard pilots her thirteen offspring through a maze of bushes, trees, and clumps of grass. Overhead, a dozen crows caw and fret in the summer sun, while the river, quiet now after the spring floods, slides by in tranquil serenity. Sandbars along the stream have been trampled by the feet of many fishermen.

It is a tranquil time before the bustle of cutting and bailing hay in the valley. The fields are green and lush, the irrigation ditches running full. The cattle have been moved into the high country, where the long grass in the meadows puts meat on their bones. Patches of melting snow send ice-cold streams rushing through the gullies to nourish flowers and grass and the wildlife of the mountains.

The energy and vitality of June and July have matured into the beauty of fulfillment. Pinecones are growing toward fruition and falling to plant new seeds for the forests of tomorrow. The haste of the early spring and summer has been abated in the tranquility of August.

Nothing can stay the march of the seasons. The chill of April and May turns to the warming sun of June and July, when nature achieves her diadem of beauty. August comes with its mellowing grace, then September and October for the harvest. It is an endless procession, replete with wonder and charm. Memory of the winter's cold is blotted out while we enjoy the lazy warmth of the summer.

The goldenrod by the roadside and the milkweed beginning to pod are reminders that the summer is on the wane. The columbine, the lovely state flower of Colorado, mostly have gone, except in the high country. The Indian paintbrush, glowing red against the green of the valley, still clings to its beauty, but the tiger lilies down by the river are growing weary. Even now, there is a foretaste of the fall.

August drones lazily, a time of pause between the freshness of spring and the harvest of fall. It is a time of deliberate ease, like retirement for a man whose real work is done. The harvest will come, but it awaits its time. Meanwhile, nature seems to rest imperceptibly from her labors, labors so dynamic and vigorous in the spring.

Vacation places are filled to the brim, as if people understood the briefness of summer's span. Campers are everywhere, lolling in the sun, fishing in the river, riding horseback into the high country, and hiking into the hidden places away from the road. Unconsciously, they are aware there is so little time for self-renewal before the summer ends.

The mood of Henry James comes naturally in the quiet hours of August. He wrote, "Summer afternoon—summer afternoon; to me those always have been the two most beautiful words in the English language." And why not? If nothing is so rare as a day in June, a balmy afternoon in August offers a similar rarity to be cherished.

Often I have wished that the lazy days of August would last a little longer. Only yesterday, we were sweeping out the summer cottage, turning on the water, raking pine needles, trimming trees, and putting the place in order. Soon we will be closing up, draining the pipes, and leaving for home. The summer will be only a precious memory, enriched by a haunting sense of gratitude.

So when the chill of September sets in, a foretaste of winter to come, fond recollections of August will cluster in mind. We will know that, in the providence of God, the seasons will roll on and August will come again.

Picnic Time

A *picnic* is defined by the dictionary as "a pleasure outing at which a meal is eaten outdoors." That is a very prosaic way of defining a picnic, which may or may not be a pleasurable experience, depending on the mood of assorted flies, mosquitoes, and bugs. The vagaries of the weather frequently conspire to ruin the pleasurable outing, so that eating outdoors leaves us rain-soaked and out of sorts.

On the whole, picnics have their points, despite some hazards. If the mosquitoes have had their fill working on previous picnickers and the weather stays pleasant, it is nice to be outdoors and away from the normal routine of things. It is enjoyable to lie in the sun awaiting refreshments while watching the birds flit happily in the trees. We have to expect, however, that the children won't allow us much time to rest in the sun.

The last time I enjoyed a picnic, it rained. The shower came up unexpectedly and without much warning just as we were sitting down around a battered table to satisfy our hunger. By the time we got into the automobile with the sandwiches and the potato chips, both had become slightly soggy, but still edible. Our clothes had become well soaked.

Happily, the shower ended in about twenty-five minutes, and the sun came out again. The grass was too wet for lolling, but a postponed softball game got under way, along with bag races and three-legged races for the children. Mothers cringed as their children slid and tumbled on the wet grass, leaving grass stains on once-clean clothing. Shoes oozed water after their baptism in numerous puddles.

As the afternoon wore on, dispositions improved, the grass

dried somewhat, and the picnic became more of a pleasurable outing. Family groups gathered to visit and to swat mosquitoes. The flies seemed to have retreated when the tables were hastily cleared during the rain. One youngster borrowed an empty pickle bottle to collect worms that had been flushed to the surface by the rain. He said his father was a fisherman.

Picnics can be fun, of course, and it would not occur to me to downgrade the pleasurable outing. When all of the conditions are right, the company altogether congenial, and the children in a cooperative frame of mind, a picnic can be a joy. I was surprised to discover, however, that almost no reputable poet has written anything about picnics. Maybe their pleasurable outings were interrupted by rain.

Picnickers have a habit of always taking too much food, with the result that we have to clean up the leftovers at home. There is something rather forlorn, however, about a day-old peanut-butter sandwich. Lettuce grows limp. Chicken legs ooze grease. Hot dogs shrivel until they are as wrinkled as prunes. It is better to gorge at the picnic than to haul the leftovers home.

Someone always brings a bat and ball to a picnic, and not-so-young fathers, remembering their athletic days, chase flies, swing the bat furiously, and run the bases as if they were twenty instead of forty or forty-five. Now, exercise, of course, is a good thing, if taken regularly. But taken in large doses at a picnic, violent exercise can have consequences. Aching muscle miseries are the usual day-after result of the pleasurable outing.

The best thing about a picnic is the laughter of the children, who seem to love the excursion into the open with their friends. They don't appear to mind the bruises and bumps that come with the games and the races. If somebody is splashed with gooey yellow in the egg-tossing contest, they love it. They fill themselves with soda pop and popcorn, unmindful of the possible aftermath. It is their day, and they make the most of it.

So, for the sake of the children, we put up with the mosquitoes and the flies and enter into their fun, playing baseball, tossing eggs, and getting splattered. If it rains we make the best of it and wait for the sun to shine. When it is over, we are inclined to remember the affair as an enjoyable outing and to forget the unpleasant episodes that were part of it.

Autumn Reveries

The mountainsides are ablaze with color, berry bushes and aspen flashing yellow and bronze, dark red and watermelon pink, against a background of green pine and spruce. Leaves from riverside willows float slowly along the now-lowered river, swimming lazily in backwaters and eddies. Sandbars and rocks, recently covered with rippling water, are bare and gray.

Hay from the valley fields, only yesterday bailed neatly in rows, has been hauled away to be stacked in the barnyard or hidden in the loft of an ample barn. After a summer grazing in the high country, the cattle are back in the valley feasting on the leftovers from the gathered hay. Their lowing breaks the silence of the early morning hours.

There is a chill in the morning air, foretelling the winter to come and the haunting sense of bitter cold yet to be. The October sun, bright in the clear blue sky, has retreated into the cosmic distance, surrendering its power to warm the earth. The squirrels have gathered nuts for their long winter sleep and put on their warmer fur coats.

Wild things of the forest have made their annual trek from the high valleys and peaks to the lower reaches, and the mallards from the canyon lake have fled south. The hummingbirds—broad-tailed hummers, ruby-throats, and rufous hummers—have made their departure. The squawking blue jays seem subdued and perhaps a little lonely.

A doe and a buck deer wandered down behind the house this morning to graze contentedly on the dwindling grass among the pines. Now and then, they lifted their graceful heads, wondering perhaps if danger lurked behind the window from which I watched. Then, seemingly reassured, they went on munching and loitering. After a while, they trotted off and disappeared among the trees on the mountainside.

In the valley beside the river, the community garden is curiously beautiful in dilapidation. Dusty brown stalks, left to stand after the corn was plucked, have the look of a drunken man in khaki trying to walk a straight line. The last of the potatoes have been dug, and wilted pea and bean vines sag against the ground. The garden gate is open, inviting invasion by raccoon, groundhog, and rabbit neighbors. The scarecrow, designed to frighten away blackbirds and crows, is somewhat the worse for the summer's wear, arms akimbo and head at a rakish angle.

It is a quiet time in the mountain valley. Summer cottagers have packed their bags, drained the house water pipes, and departed for their winter's toil in the city. Traffic on the highway has dwindled to a trickle, the bumper-to-bumper snarls of the summer only a memory. The few who remain in the valley have their woodpiles stacked high ready for the coming cold.

October stars are bright in the bowl of the sky when the night closes in, and half-seen clouds break the patterns of Pegasus and the Big Dipper. Lights flicker below from the windows of neighbors to banish fear of the dark. Outside my bedroom window, a friendly owl, perched in a tall pine, makes his presence known, as he has done for months on end.

The pageantry of the seasons is afoot, like a woman changing her raiment from summer to autumn. The land will lie fallow now, regaining its strength for the spring. There are patches of snow on the peaks, white as billowing sheets in the wind, waiting there for the thaw of the spring. The many-colored leaves will fall to nourish the earth, and needles from pines and spruces will carpet the forest floor to protect the seedling trees.

The seasonal drama is implicit in the economy of God, meant to refurbish the land and make it fruitful again. "October's bright blue weather" is but one facet of the march of time, repeated over and over through the years. Only God could transform my valley from the myriad colors of autumn to the lush, alive beauty of the spring yet to come.

Faith to Live By

God, though this life is but a wraith,
Although we know not what we use,
Although we grope with little faith,
Give me the heart to fight—and lose.

. . . .

From compromise and things half done
Keep me, with stern and stubborn pride;
And when, at last, the fight is won,
God keep me still unsatisfied.

"Prayer" by LOUIS UNTERMEYER

Vein of Iron

There is a sentence in Rudyard Kipling's oft-quoted poem "If" that is worth remembering in a time of recession and disappointment:

> If you can...
> ... watch the things you gave your life to, broken,
> And stoop and build 'em up with worn-out tools:
>
> .   .   .   .
>
> ... you'll be a man, ...

Ours is a day of broken dreams and frustrated hopes that requires courage to build again with "worn-out tools."

These days call us to search for the vein of iron in the American character. We have discerned it before in times of stress and uncertainty, and with ingenuity, courage, and faith, we have surmounted our ills. We will do so again, if we have not grown too soft and flabby through times of affluence and comfort.

It was Henry David Thoreau who wrote of "3-o'clock-in-the-morning courage" (which Napoleon thought was the rarest), but Thoreau cherished a long-range courage that "sleeps only when the storm sleeps" and goes on toiling and believing as long as the storm rages. It is the long-range courage Thoreau honored that is needed now.

As we enter the third century of our nation, memories of the past should inspire confidence in the future. There were men who, like George Washington, Thomas Jefferson, and James Madison, staked their lives and their sacred honor on what appeared to be a lost cause. The might of the British Empire was ranged against them, and they would have lost the struggle for independence except for the vein of iron in them that refused to buckle under all that might.

The agony of the Civil War brought the nation to its knees, and, for a time, its future hung in the balance. But, out of the ashes, there arose ultimately a nation united and on the march to a future brighter than anyone could have imagined. There was something more than "3-o'clock-in-the-morning courage" that carried the nation through its time of peril.

There is a strange paradox in the fact that, without great agony, there is no great music; without pain, there is no progress; without suffering, there is no splendor. Harsh circumstances have a way of revealing the vein of iron that is in us. H. G. Wells pictured the alternative in his portrait of a scientifically designed Utopia, which his hero leaves with the lament, "What have I done to be sent to a realm where everything is provided for a man, and only his heart and his hope and his spirit are taken from him?"

Obviously, we are far from Utopia, and many of our dreams have fallen into ruin. In many respects, we share the experience of Sir Winston Churchill after one of his numerous failures on the road to triumph. "I returned to London," he wrote, "with those feelings of deflation which a bottle of champagne or even soda water represents when it has been half-emptied and left uncorked for a night."

Nevertheless, the courage that persists until "the storm sleeps" kept Churchill going and led him to his victories. He may well have remembered the instructions that Comte Henri de Saint-Simon, the articulate exponent of a positive philosophy, gave to his valet. Each morning, the valet was to address him, "Remember, Monsieur le Comte, that you have great things to do."

No matter how dark the night or how severe the storm, we have great things to do. It is no time to sit in sad inertia, bent in sorrow like a weeping willow tree. We may have to learn how to put up with hard times while we are seeking to discover how to emerge out of the valley and into the sunlight on the other side. We may need to do without some things while we are learning to climb out of the chasm into which we have fallen.

The future will be bright, however, if we rediscover the vein of iron that is in us and carry on with something more than "3-o'clock-in-the-morning courage."

100

Trifocal Vision

When my oculist suggested some years ago that I ought to have bifocals, I protested. He smiled knowingly and remarked that eyestrain added to age resulted in a need for bifocals. "But," I said, "I'm not that old yet." He just grinned and gave me a prescription for bifocals.

Wearing my bifocals, I set out for my vacation and promptly found one good use for the near-vision lens. I could thread a number 14 trout fly without innumerable false thrusts, after the fashion of an amateur trying to thread a needle. That made me a bifocal convert. On the other hand, bifocals can be a hazard. A woman I know got bifocals and promptly fell down the stairs. The steps were out of focus. All she saw was a blur and down she went.

Obviously, it is fatal to look at distant things through a near-vision lens. That obscures the long view and puts it out of focus. Someone said of a man of literary note, "His eyes are fashioned for small contempts." Preoccupied with little problems and trivial matters nearby, life was as small as the near-vision lens through which he saw it. So, as Matthew Arnold said, life was "a long headache on a noisy street."

Sir Hugh Walpole said that there are three horizons with which both literature and life must deal. Having come now to the age of trifocals, I am prepared to accept this notion. The first horizon, says Walpole, is the immediate scene, your street and my street, and our little day-to-day problems. The second horizon is the world situation, with all the issues that concern the world and the nation on our divided and confused planet. The third horizon is the cosmic one, in which the eternal issues of right and wrong, good and evil, and the ultimates of meaning and value are to be found.

There are some people who live mostly on the first horizon, seeing life through near-vision lenses. Immersed in their own little concerns and beset by problems of getting and spending, they are "fashioned for small contempts" and small troubles. They plod through the years with their eyes on their feet. Their ceiling is zero, and trivial problems leave them bewildered and saying, What's the use?

More men and women, I suspect, add the second horizon to the first. They see not only the immediate scene but also the national and international panorama that forms the framework for their lives. Unfortunately, when things look black and unpromising on the second horizon, intermediate vision is by no means enough. There is no hope or promise anywhere to be seen, and we come to the view of Ma Joad in John Steinbeck's *Grapes of Wrath*, "There ain't nothin' a body can trust no more."

Hope, courage, and faith for great living are to be found on the third horizon, where we confront the abiding values that will not fail, even though "the earth be shaken into the midst of the sea." Looking toward the far horizon, where the judgments of God are "sure and righteous altogether," we know that tyranny stands on feet of clay, and evil, in the end, destroys itself. On the far horizon, there are inner resources with which to meet the problems of the first and second horizons with wisdom and courage.

I'm in favor of trifocals for life, especially if they invite us to lift up our eyes unto the hills "whence cometh our strength."

Cope with Your Tears

One of my correspondents wrote to me a little while ago to ask, "How can I cope with the loss of the one with whom I shared life for more than forty years?" The question may seem exotic in an age of divorce and marital conflict. It is important, however, for the many who have lived and worked, laughed and cried, together through years of comradeship.

Coping with what Virgil called "the tears in things" is not easy. Even though we know that, sooner or later, we will be separated from those with whom we have shared our joys and sorrows, the poignancy of separation still is acute when it comes. We feel something of "the tragic sense of life," as Miguel de Unamuno called it, that leaves us alone and lonely. The familiar patterns of life are abruptly altered.

Sorrow and grief are among life's inevitables and we cannot run away from them. When loss comes, it is not wise to bury our heads in the sand and pretend our grief does not exist. When we are left alone, we have no choice except to face our aloneness and come to terms with it. It is good to let the tears flow and to feel what we ought to feel.

When grief is bottled inside, presenting a stiff upper lip to the world, both healing and adjustment are delayed. It is better to think it out and talk it out, expressing honest emotions, until we are free to face the future and deal with it understandingly. Once we are able to confront openly the stark pain of reality and the full implication of our loss, we are ready to begin the long process of adjusting to our new estate.

Having faced the reality of loss, the corollary necessity is to accept it. To be resentful or rebellious is to compound misery.

When Margaret Fuller, one of the Boston Transcendentalists, remarked, "I accept life," Ralph Waldo Emerson responded, "By gad, she'd better." So we had better accept life, our grief and our tears, or there can be no healing for our hurt.

Heaven only knows what an anonymous poet had experienced before writing:

> Keep me from bitterness. It is so easy
> To nurse sharp, bitter thoughts each dull, dark hour,
> Against self-pity, Man of Sorrows, defend me,
> With Thy deep sweetness and Thy gentle power.

It is easy to nurse "bitter thoughts" when those who are dearest to us slip from our grasp. But, in bitterness, there is no help.

In the hour that we face our grief and accept it, we discover there are spiritual resources to bear us to creative adjustment. The New Testament promises comfort to the grief-stricken. The word *comfort* comes from the two Latin words *con* and *fortis*. Literally, the combination means "strengthened by being with." So, comfort is not a sentimental affair. It is a reinforcing of the heart with strength and courage from life's spiritual depths.

There is light for our darkness and strength for our weakness, for we are not alone. A lovely old Jewish hymn has the truth:

> Every tear on earth that flows,
> God the ruler surely knows.

That is the affirmation, too, of the Christian faith, made regnant on a cross. God is in the midst of us, in our suffering and grief, not to explain it, but to share it.

God is mindful of the tears that flow and, in a hundred ways, He comes to share the hurt. He comes through the ministry of others, and He comes in the inner sanctuaries, where we wait for His comfort and His peace. When He comes, we are not afraid or bitter or resentful.

A thoughtful woman remarked after suffering a traumatic loss, "I learned to use my agony and to make it work for me." She used it, after facing and coming to terms with her loss, by committing herself to the ongoing tasks of life. She learned to share the tears of those she knew and to lend her understanding to their need. She found that "the tears in things" in her own life made her sensitive to the tears of others and creatively helpful. She used her own agony magnificently.

Relax, but Don't Be Lax

It is curious the way our anxieties increase with our affluence. In all logic, it ought to be the other way around. Having succeeded greatly, we occupy a hard-won pedestal, but the moment we are on top, we begin to worry that somebody will push us off. Having won economic prestige, we become anxious lest we lose it.

Anybody who has visited the offices of a stockbroker during a serious decline in stock values could feel the horrible anxiety and fear present. There is a haunting, terrible concern lest wealth and security be lost. Some are on the verge of panic. Life and horizons close in, and nothing really matters, except what is happening on the floors of the stock exchanges.

The fear we feel at the prospect of loss is understandable. What is cause for more concern, however, is the loss of equanimity. Notice the word *equanimity*. It comes from the two Latin words *aequus*, meaning "equal," and *animus*, meaning "mind." It suggests "evenness of mind, calmness, composure of mind, not easily agitated by good or ill fortune." Nevertheless, in moments of threatened loss, we are frightfully agitated and anxious. We cannot even comprehend the possibility of loss without having nervous jitters.

Jesus was aware that there is no security for anybody in the realm of secular values. He knew something of the history of His own people—how succeeding invasions had swept over their land. The rich had become poor overnight, and economic values had been swept away with the wind and the tide. What is more, there would be other invasions and other disasters. Possessions, Jesus knew, could not sustain the souls of men and women.

My mind goes back to the days of the Great Depression, when millions lost everything. I saw men and women coming apart at

105

the seams, both morally and spiritually. I saw something else, too. I saw love binding families together in mutual trust, sustaining them and helping them find values they had never known before.

I recall one elderly couple, accepting the loss of all they owned, yet saying, "We still have everything as long as we have each other." I witnessed a community coming together in the spirit of "one for all and all for one." Qualities of human compassion, long dormant, came to the fore and made life not only endurable but also very rich and rewarding. I came to understand what Jesus meant when He said: "Man shall not live by bread alone."

We live in the kind of world in which loss is possible, so we had best come to terms with realities and learn that we can find values to compensate for loss.

There is, I think, a valid suggestion for the relief of anxious minds in a highway sign erected for traveling motorists. It reads, Relax, But Don't Be Lax.

To relax means, among other things, to make less rigid and less tense and to release from strain. So relax with trust in God but don't be lax or careless.

Problems on Our Hands

Most of us wish we had fewer problems on our hands. We would like to relax and let life happen to us pleasantly. Realistically, though, we find ourselves in briar patches more often than in beds of roses. But perhaps we should be grateful that the world "is a vale of soul-making" in which character can be bred. Coriolanus, in Shakespeare's play, comments with gentle irony:

> When the sea was calm, all boats alike
> Show'd mastership in floating.

Stormy weather shows the difference between "mastership in floating" and weakness in the hull.

A disturbed man, panic in his voice, reviewed a succession of unfortunate experiences that had left him broke and jobless. The events had wounded his spirit and left him without enthusiasm for life. He ended by saying, "Things have just fallen apart." After floating along comfortably in calm weather, he had met a storm that brought him close to sinking.

It is not difficult to identify with that distraught man. Ours is a time when youth is tempted to lose heart; the old feel betrayed; and the middle-aged are bogged down. Cynicism tempts our minds, and hope seems remote. Obviously, ours is not a predictable world. It is a world of risk, where nothing is certain but the unexpected and, as someone said, where prudence lies in "the masterly administration of the unforeseen."

We may complain that this is a terrible world. Socrates might have made the same complaint. The prophets noted that the world was in a bad way, and Jesus met its grim reality. The world plainly is "a vale of soul-making" and not a Utopia. In this world,

107

the only one we have, there is no progress without struggle. We can't have crops without plowing the ground, birth without pain, or growth without challenge and response. But this world poses a challenge to our creativity, an invitation to our inventiveness, and a claim to our courage.

Many of us have found that faith is the indispensable ingredient in responding to challenge. It is not a matter of believing in God as a cosmic bellhop waiting in the wings to carry our baggage and make things comfortable for us. On the contrary, as Samuel Miller wrote: "Faith faces everything that makes the world uncomfortable—pain, fear, loneliness, shame, death—and acts with a compassion by which these things are transformed, even exalted. At the very point where atheism seems most reasonable, perhaps inevitable, faith affirms the reality of God."

Faith to Abbé Pierre is "penicillin" for despair, which he declared to be the world's worst illness. Faith steadied Ezekiel, exiled in Babylon, and enabled him to say, "The spirit entered into me . . . and set me on my feet." It inspired the Psalmist, facing evil men, and led him to write: "The Lord is my light and my salvation; whom shall I fear? The Lord is the strength of my life; of whom shall I be afraid?" It stirred the spirit of Isaiah, confronting national disaster, and led him to assert, "They that wait upon the Lord shall renew their strength." It came to Paul, facing situations that would have defeated most of us, and he was "strengthened with might, through His spirit in the inner man."

These men of faith showed "mastership in floating," not in calm seas, but in stormy weather. When things seemed to have fallen apart, they stood erect and were voices of confidence and hope to inspire a faltering people. They were not just whistling in the dark to keep up their failing spirits. On the contrary, they had found something solid and dependable that enabled them to act with courage and hope.

The ages are filled with the names of men of faith who helped to stabilize the times in which they lived and left a legacy of hope for us—Augustine, Francis Xavier, and Martin Luther. Their lives show us how to face our problems with dignity, courage, and hope born of faith in God.

The Last of Life

As we journey through the sunset years of our lives, old friends and loved ones drop off like the brown leaves on a tree in the fall. Their passing occasions vacant places in our lives and a sense of nostalgia for our yesterdays. The past, peopled with cherished faces, lives in memory, but it is not easy to adjust to their absence from the now. Nevertheless, we know we have no choice but to take each day as it comes with whatever courage and grace we can muster to mitigate our sense of loss.

We wish we could say with Robert Browning's Rabbi Ben Ezra:

> Grow old along with me!
> The best is yet to be,
> The last of life, for which the first was made.

We are not really persuaded, though, that the good rabbi was right in his judgment of old age. We suspect that our future is mostly in the past. The world soon will forget the laurels we won and the achievements of our younger days. It is a little hard to take when youth sniffs at our hard-earned wisdom.

An old man, looking at the scrapbook of his accomplishments compiled by his wife, remarked with a wry smile, "My grandchildren are not interested in the least." They have their friends, their activities, their future, and grandpa's exploits seem pale in the light of their own concerns. Someday, maybe, they will understand and be grateful for their goodly heritage.

There are compensations, of course, for the later years, especially if we are fortunate enough to have the mates of the years beside us. Mellowed by the years, we find deep joy in being together. It is a joy to see our children assuming responsibility in the world and making places for themselves. It is fun to watch our grandchildren growing up and our children plowing ideals and values into their lives the way we tried to do long ago. It provides a sense of meaning for our lives and gives weight to the conviction that our struggles really were worthwhile.

It is something of a relief, too, when we don't have to fight the rush-hour traffic day after day. If it is pouring rain outside, we don't have to make a wet dash for the 7:30 train bound for town. In some ways, we miss the tension and the pressure we knew in our younger days, the office politics and even the feuds, but we are grateful for quietness and a chance to meditate and think.

We are free now to do some of the things we always said we would like to do: to read the books we never got around to reading, to see the places we thought we would like to see, and to putter with making things in a do-it-yourself way.

We know, in a dim sort of way, that sooner or later we will have to go it alone, without the ones we have loved the most. That possibility has been there from the beginning, even though we have resisted thinking about it. Grief and loss are among life's inevitables to be managed with maturity and faith. The old slogan of the theater "The show must go on" is pertinent. Life will go on with dignity if we know that, "in the valley of the shadow," we are not alone. God is there to lend us His strength.

Usually, I suspect, we respond to the inevitables of old age the way we always have responded to hard blows and hurts. If we had resilience at twenty-five, we will have it at seventy as well. If we knew how to cope with disappointment at thirty, we will manage it at sixty-five. If we were able to adjust to hard situations when we were younger, we will cope with loss and grief with quiet courage in the sunset years. Life has a pattern that holds through the years and, as it was said of Bobby Burns, "He was a makin' himself a' the time, but he dinna ken what he was about until the years had passed."

Essentially, I suspect, Rabbi Ben Ezra was right. We can make the most of the last of life if we know down deep inside that

> Our times are in His hand,
> Who saith "A whole I planned,"
> Youth shows but half; trust God; see all nor be afraid.

Don't Push the River

Most of us are impatient. We want to make things happen. We push when we ought to relax and let things happen in their own good time. A wise psychiatrist advised, "Don't push the river; it flows by itself." Nevertheless, we are disposed to force issues without seeking a consensus, and to press for decisions without waiting to assess all the available evidence. We try to push the unpushable.

Much of the agony and woe of our times is the consequence of our impatience for immediate results. We are victims of motion without meditation and drive without direction. Long ago, in the days before automobiles, airplanes, and high-speed trains enabled us to go nowhere faster than ever before, Elizabeth Fry, the Quaker ambassadress of God, was greatly troubled by the driving speed of the new world. She felt what she called "a degradation of the inner life."

There has been an acceleration of that "degradation of the inner life" in our time. We have no wish to be alone with our thoughts, to think things through so that we can flow with the river in dealing with the issues in our lives. We prefer to go somewhere, to do something, anything, to avoid thoughtful analysis of our situation.

It is a curious matter, but we seem to have the feeling that it is a disgrace not to be, or to seem to be, frightfully busy and perpetually under pressure. We seldom are willing to admit we have time on our hands. It would be in poor taste to make such an admission. We prefer to be busy, with no time to think or meditate, even though, as a consequence, we make stupid mistakes.

Wisdom and judgment that lead us to flow with the river are born in quiet places. The times of quiet may seem to be unproductive, but as Dwight Moody said, "A bath isn't lasting, but it does you good to take one now and then." Times of quietness are surprisingly refreshing, providing a sense of direction and purpose to our lives.

The scriptural admonition "be still and know" makes good sense. We cannot really know in any other way. To be sure, we learn by experience, or do we? The incessantly active moth, flying into the camp lantern, singeing its wings, and then burning to death in the end, learns nothing from its tilts with the flame. What we learn from the pain of our burns is a consequence of our reflection. Hurt once, we reason then that we may be hurt again.

It is in the moments of meditation after experience that we learn or fail to learn the meaning of our hurt. Burned by fire, we learn fast; but burned by our moral failures we digest the meaning of our experience with incredible reluctance. Why? Partly, at least, because we use furious activity as a means of stifling thought and massacring meditation. It hurts too much to think, so we run away madly. We go on pushing the river as if we could stop its flowing.

It is only by way of honest meditation that we translate our hurts, our failures, and our mistakes into growing points. When Henry David Thoreau found his life one succession of disappointments after another, he understood the necessity for quietness. "I seek a garret," he said to Ralph Waldo Emerson, and, then, because members of his family invaded his garret sanctuary, he went to Walden Pond. He went, he said, "to find himself." He left for us the rich bequest of what he had found—the mellowed wisdom and the sound judgment of stillness. "Be still and know" was a text Thoreau understood profoundly.

Quite simply put, we grow in wisdom and judgment only when we are quiet enough to hear "the still, small voice" of God. We cannot manage God, whose power flows like a river. He cannot be pushed or coerced. "If the vision tarry," we had better "wait for it" or risk the peril of pushing on blindly.

The contemporary interest in transcendental meditation suggests we may have come around to the ancient insight calling us to "be still and know." If we have come to the point of knowing we can't push the river, we are on the road to deeper wisdom and peace of mind. We have found a balm for our pain.

Prayer and Action

A passage in Exodus portrays Moses and his people complaining of their lot as they flee from the pursuing Egyptians. God then says to Moses, "Why do you cry unto me? Tell the people to go forward." Or, as the Living Bible Version puts it, "Stop praying and start marching."

Prayer, the passage suggests, is not a substitute for action but an integral part of it. If prayer becomes merely an excuse for not doing what we ought to do, it is time to "stop praying and start marching." Prayer is "the soul's sincere desire," which may be "uttered or unexpressed," but it is significant only when offered with supportive action.

Ralph Waldo Emerson may have overemphasized action when he insisted that the prayers God hears are those of "the rower bending to his oar" and of "the farmer sowing seed." But he was trying to say that doing and praying ought to move in the same direction. If prayer is only a semantic exercise devoid of purposeful activity designed to translate the desires of prayer into reality, it is sterile.

Jesus retreated into secluded places to pray for guidance, but He always returned to the city to minister with the wisdom gained in prayer. He climbed up to mountain heights to meditate and to pray, but He returned to the marketplace "in the power of the Spirit" and went about doing good in response to God's will as discerned in prayer.

Most of us, I suspect, pray too little. We have an activist temperament and are inclined to equate goodness with much movement from place to place. As the Reverend George Tyrrell once remarked, "It is our feeling that Christianity consists of going

113

about doing good, especially the kind of doing good which involves a great deal of going about." We find it difficult to punctuate our activity with "pregnant pauses" for prayer.

Both prayer and action are important. We cannot act and forget to pray or pray and neglect to act. Moses and his people apparently did plenty of praying but couldn't bear marching on toward freedom, so the command they heard to "stop praying and start marching" was altogether appropriate.

Action inspired by prayer is dynamic and purposeful. It is no accident that William Wilberforce and the men who worked with him for the abolition of the slave trade were men of prayer. Neither is it surprising that General William Booth, who founded the Salvation Army, was a man of prayer.

Prayerful faith creates men and women who can be trusted with social tasks and without whom dreams of social progress and of the good society never can come to fulfillment. The glory and the power of prayer is to be seen in the lives of people who can be trusted and whose selfless character provides the brick and mortar for a better world.

We become that for which we pray with our whole being. To verbalize in prayer but make no provision for action is to pervert prayer. Prayers that are merely words develop the explosive power of damp cement. We become like the famous congregation in Samuel Butler's *Way of All Flesh:* "equally shocked at hearing Christianity denied or at seeing it practiced."

The Scriptures note that King Amaziah of Judah "did what was right, but sometimes resented it." It is better, I suspect, to do right and to resent having to do it than to do wrong. Nevertheless, resentfully doing right suggests a divided personality struggling against itself, not a spirit "like a strong, steady wind that blows one way."

In the same fashion, prayer for the good we really do not want leaves us unable to act with resolution and courage. But when we wholeheartedly wish the good for which we pray, we find a plus added to our efforts "by the courtesy of God." Prayer means power when it enlists the whole self in creative action.

Truth Comes in Stillness

Finding quietness in a world geared to noise and activity is something of a problem. After listening for some weeks to the hammers and drills of workmen building an apartment, one woman remarked, "I just can't stand the noise another day." But, paradoxically, we can't stand stillness, either. A young woman put the truth wisely when she said of her father, "He just can't stand it to be still. The moment I get home, he wants to play bridge or canasta." So, on one hand, we can't stand noise and, on the other, we can't stand silence.

The blunt truth, however, is that our capacity to endure the noise and the fury of the world around us depends upon our ability to enjoy quietness. The resources of the stillness enable us to meet the strain of noise and drive. If we can't stand it to be still, neither can we move wisely or serenely through the noise and strain of life. If we do not stop to be still, we can't stand it to keep going, for it is in the stillness that we find wisdom and strength for pushing on.

Wisdom for life comes from silent places, and we need to be wise. A man has to be still to know anything. T. S. Eliot says we are the "hollow men," with our "heads stuffed with straw," because we cannot endure the quietness of creative thought. Our ivory towers have turned into bridge clubs. We have no time for listening to the thundering truths that come to us in stillness.

The problem of our noisy, turbulent era is to create an atmosphere for listening. A good friend of mine tells me that he sometimes makes a date with himself for lunch. He finds a table in a peaceful corner of a restaurant and spends the lunch hour quietly thinking. To be sure, knives and forks rattle around him

115

and the hum of busy conversation surges in the room. But my friend is silent, alone with his thoughts, and quite content to be so. Let it be noted that ideas thunder through the silence he has created for himself.

God speaks to our minds if we create an atmosphere for listening. William Blake felt the truth when insights flashed from nowhere to enrich his writing. "It is not mine! It is not mine," he said. In scientific research, there are flashes of insight that come like thunder into the silence of brooding meditation. Heimholtz noted of one of his discoveries, "It was given to me." No doubt it was. The mystics always have contended rightly that God reveals His truth to those who wait in quietness.

A wise one observes that "modern man is suffering from degradation of the inner life." An Arab guide noted as much when the muezzin in his minaret called Jerusalem to the hour of prayer. It seemed strange to hear the muezzin speaking the ancient summons with the help of a modern loudspeaker. We saw no one who stopped to pray according to the Muslim custom. Our guide, noting our wonder, remarked, "Unfortunately, this is not the golden age of prayer."

I suspect the agony of our era, our confusion and bewildering conflicts, can be traced to the simple fact that not only in the Muslim world but also in Christendom "this is not the golden age of prayer." On the contrary, it is the age of activity and anxiety, of revolution and regret. The degradation of the inner life has brought with it a degeneration of political, social, and economic life. It has brought in its wake a loss of poise and patience.

Yet, even now, it is not too late to "be still and know that I am God" and so to find both wisdom and stability for life in our noisy, turbulent world.

One Day at a Time

Our complex world generates tension. Under various stresses, especially that of competition, we are inclined to feel strained and taut. Franz Alexander in *Our Age of Unreason* sees "his patients—physicians, lawyers, engineers, bankers, advertising men, teachers and laboratory-research men of the universities, students, and clerks—engaged in a marathon race." He says, "They would all like to stop but dare not as long as the others are running."

In our mad scramble to climb the ladder of success, we have little time for the friendliness and neighborliness that are so essential to healthy minds. We blunder into a compulsive pattern of competitive hostility that defies our capacity to relax and to find the fluid generosities of friendship and love.

The young executive, aware that recession has placed his job in jeopardy, pushes himself relentlessly. His anxieties imperil his judgment, and his tensions magnify small matters out of all proportion. He is a prisoner of his success at the same time that he feels threatened by the possibility of losing it. Work becomes his passion, and his wife becomes bored to tears at his side.

There are times, of course, when tension releases vital energies that enable us to think clearly and act wisely. But creative tension is possible only when it emerges out of the comfortable flow of a well-ordered life. The body consumes energy when it is under tension; it restores energy when it is relaxed. Unrelieved tension drains resources of mind and body at a rate that cannot be sustained for long.

If we live wisely, alternating periods of tension with times of relaxation, we can constantly restore and replenish our energy reserves. If, on the other hand, we live under constant tension and anxiety, we begin to suffer from fatigue and persistent tiredness.

Under persistent tension, we become less and less able to cope with whatever we are doing. Our minds are jaded by the unremitting stress we feel. Our bodies refuse to provide the energy our tasks demand. We invite precisely what we fear the most.

Gertrude Lawrence expressed the skill of a competent actress and the strength of a fine person when she was on the stage. She also was aware of the tension of performing before an audience. One clue to her stability and poise is suggested by a card she kept on her dressing table. It read: "Anyone can carry his burden, however heavy, till nightfall. Anyone can do his work, however hard, for one day. Short horizons make life easier and give us one of the blessed secrets of brave, true, holy living."

An octogenarian who lived through the Great Depression, two world wars, and assorted personal difficulties summed up the truth of the matter by noting, "Inch by inch, life is a cinch; yard by yard, life is hard." Most of our tensions come from adding the anxieties of the future to the burdens of the present. Inch by inch, however, we can manage.

Many of us have learned that by taking one day at a time and refusing to confuse the present moment with tomorrow's worries, we can cope competently with the eternal now. It is a matter of faith, I think, of believing that if we carry whatever loads we must through the day, we can safely leave tomorrow to God. Tomorrow may be tough and disappointing, but, with both courage and wisdom, we can manage it when it comes.

The distinguished philosopher Charles Morris described the need for "proper detachments and proper attachments"—that is to say, proper attachments to the tasks of the moment and proper detachments from the problems of tomorrow. Like Spinoza, he would look at things "under the aspect of eternity" and see both the present and the future in perspective. Undergirded by faith in God, he could take the small moment of the present in his stride and, quietly relaxed, see it "under the aspect of eternity."

Things to Remember

Joys too exquisite to last,
And yet more exquisite when past.

.   .   .   .

Remembered joys are never past;
At once the fountain, stream and sea,
They were, they are, they yet shall be.

"The Little Cloud"
by JAMES MONTGOMERY

A Bit of Nostalgia

Riding the seldom-on-time narrow-gauge railroad from Denver to Shawnee, Colorado, is one of my earliest boyhood memories. It was an adventure of major proportions for a youngster to board a little railroad coach behind old Number 9 and chug up Platte Canyon. The roaring river in the canyon provided a musical accompaniment for the clatter of the train.

When the car windows were opened in the summertime to provide relief from the stifling heat, cinders from Number 9 flew through the windows and into the car. A cinder lodged in the eye was an unpleasant experience. The candy man, a basket slung from his neck, offered candy and chewing gum, along with cheerful banter, to small boys and adults, while the train made its way up the canyon at twenty to thirty miles an hour.

The narrow-gauge railroad, originally known as the Denver, South Park, and Pacific, was the brainchild of Governor John Evans of Colorado. He later founded Evanston, Illinois, and Northwestern University. Known as "Napoleon" Evans because of his organizational genius, Evans envisioned a railroad reaching from Denver to the Pacific. Building got under way in 1873, and the rails, only three feet apart, were laid up Platte Canyon, through South Platte, Bailey, and Grant, over Kenosha Pass, and to Como in South Park.

When gold was discovered in Leadville, Jay Gould, the New York financier, acquired controlling interest in the road and diverted it to Leadville by way of Buena Vista. Later, to shorten the distance to Leadville, the rails were pushed over Boreas Pass, through Breckenridge, and over Mosquito Pass to Leadville. Through the 1880s, the South Park hauled millions of dollars in gold from Leadville to Denver. It carried such passengers as President Ulysses Grant, Oscar Wilde, and Horace Tabor and his wife, Baby Doe, on its well-appointed sleeping cars.

The fishermen's trains did a roaring business in the 1890s and on into the 1900s, running between Denver and Grant. Whenever a fisherman wished to be dropped off at his favorite haunt, the train would stop. Every mile or so, a fisherman would disembark, set up his rod, and begin casting for trout. If he was lucky, he had a lean-to or a cabin in which to spend the night. The next day, all he had to do to get back to Denver was to step up to the right-of-way and wave a handkerchief at the engineer. Often, there were two or three fish trains on Saturdays and Sundays during the summer months.

In the 1930s, the days of the narrow gauge were coming to an end. Automobiles, trucks, and a broad-gauge line into Leadville signaled the demise of the South Park. It hung on for a time, but on August 10, 1937, the Denver-to-Leadville service ceased, and, in the 1940s, when metals were scarce because of World War II, the tracks were uprooted and resmelted for the war effort.

The quiet, little valley of the Platte has changed, given way, I suppose, to progress. Cars, campers, and trucks roar up and down the highway, bumper to bumper on weekends. Property values and taxes have multiplied as real-estate developers have turned mountainsides into sites for cottages and condominiums.

Old-timers lament the passing of the way things were when the little railroad traversed the canyon and the valley. They remember old Number 9 puffing and sputtering on its way. Their nostalgia is akin to that of Emily Dickinson, who wrote of a train:

> I like to see it lap the miles,
> And lick the valleys up,
> And stop to feed itself at tanks.

Something of the beauty and romance of the past is gone, but more people are enjoying the outdoors, building cabins, and camping beneath snow-capped peaks. Perhaps it is better the way it is now—I am not sure. But when great trees go down to make way for mountain villages, when beer cans, pop bottles, and other waste clutter the scenery, I think of the admonition expressed by an anonymous poet:

> Let no one say, and say it to your shame,
> That all was beauty here until you came.

An Old-fashioned Word

There is an old-fashioned word my grandmother used that I haven't heard for a long time. The word is *mettle*. It means courage and even more than courage. It is an ingrained capacity to bear up under strain after the fashion of a finely tempered steel blade. To be on one's mettle is to be aroused or prepared to do one's best with spirit, courage, and ardor.

Life is not an everlasting picnic in perfect weather. On the contrary, it is a matter of struggle, a mixture of triumph and failure, joy and sorrow. It takes mettle to keep on going when circumstances conspire to thwart our hopes and aspirations, to meet strain in the heat of battle and then to wait for the final verdict. As a Persian poet wrote long ago:

> It was not in the open battle
> We threw away our swords.
> It was in the darkness, waiting
> By the waters of the fords.

Most of us find it difficult to wait when a conspiracy of obstacles stands in our way. Nevertheless, as Ralph Waldo Emerson wrote to Thomas Carlyle, "The sphere of opportunities opens slowly." It always is a long road to travel from where we are to where we want to be. We begin with the spirit of the young, as James Russell Lowell sang, "with rays of morn on their white Shields of Expectation," but progress is slow and tortuous.

Waiting is an art that our impatient days have forgotten. So, when our progress is slow we begin to wonder if it makes sense to go on trying. It is the capacity to go on and on, however, giving one's best through the long days and months and years of waiting, that is the mark of character and mettle.

The triumphant spirits of the world are those who honorably accept the challenges laid down to them. They refuse to be stopped by difficulties. They possess the kind of courage that Emerson defines in his essay "Circles" as the "power of self-recovery," so that "a man cannot have his flank turned, cannot be out-generaled, but put him where you will, he stands."

When a man has mettle like that, obstacles become stepping-stones. Even his defeats are made useful to him, and he draws strength from his weakness. Like "the wounded oyster, [he] mends his shell with pearl." In fact, ease is inimical to growth, while struggle through hardship and discouragement leads to maturity of mind and spirit.

In a time of economic dislocation such as we have known in recent years, the dreams of many have been smashed. A young Ph.D., driving a taxi because he could not find a job as a chemist, remarked: "This job will keep me afloat until something opens up for me. I'm still young; I can afford to wait." He was not bitter or resentful. On the contrary, he was making the best of a bad situation.

Nathaniel Hawthorne, who traveled a different road before he found the key to triumph, wrote a sentence significant for all whose dreams are temporarily at bay. He was writing for the benefit of artists, and Herman Melville underlined the words in his copy of *The Artist and the Beautiful*. Hawthorne wrote, "He [the artist] must keep his faith in himself while the incredulous world assails him with its utter disbelief."

That, I suspect, is where all of us have to begin when our hopes are thwarted. Faith in ourselves is one thing we never can afford to surrender. It is the key to mettle, to courage to keep on going when we feel drained. When we cease to believe in ourselves and our God-given powers and possibilities, we are finished. It is the man who can go on believing "in himself while the incredulous world assails him with its utter disbelief" who comes through undefeated, the wounds in his "shell" mended "with pearl."

These are times to test the mettle of us all.

Bound in Shallows

Shakespeare might well have been speaking to us today when he wrote in *Julius Caesar:*

> There is a tide in the affairs of men,
> Which, taken at the flood, leads on to fortune;
> Omitted, all the voyage of their life
> Is bound in shallows and miseries.

Such a tide is upon us now. At home and abroad, the old order has been swept away, and we are feeling the birth pangs of the new, not yet fully born. "The shape of things to come" is in our hands, and, as Louis Adamic wrote, "We need to realize as quickly as possible that this crisis is not so much a crisis as a rare and enormous opportunity."

An opportunity presents at one and the same time both peril and promise. It is a grave peril if we are not prepared spiritually and intellectually to make the most of it, but it is a promise laden with possibilities if we are ready to seize it in God's name and turn it to the world's account and ours.

There is a radical turn of mind, radical in the sense that it habitually strikes at the roots of issues and problems, which is an urgent necessity if we are to seize the tide of our time and find our way beyond the sterility of conflict to creative growth. Our superficial thinking, "bound in the shallows" the way it is, has turned life into a farce or a comedy, when, as Miguel de Unamuno, the Spanish philosopher, noted, it is a tragedy. By that, he means that life makes sense and we reap what we sow.

A farce, as someone noted, is a play in which the plot hinges on accidents. If a man stubs his toe, falls out of bed, or gets on a train going the wrong way by mistake, the event may be very funny, but it does not follow from any moral failure in the man.

A tragedy, however, is different. It is a play in which effect follows cause, and things happen for discernible reasons. Hamlet, Macbeth, and King Lear met disaster because progressive deterioration of character in each of them made death inevitable.

Our contemporary crisis is in the nature of tragedy, and simply to blame our plight on the government, business, or Communism is to turn tragedy into burlesque and to miss the fact that the moral illness of civilization is the root cause of our ills.

If there is logic in life, as any thoughtful person must see there is, then our illness has gone beyond the help of superficial remedies. We will not be saved by Utopian panaceas suggested by politicians courting votes. Nothing less than a moral revolution striking at the base of our sickness can save us.

We may tinker with economic systems, international organizations, or social security programs, but we will get nowhere until we experience a moral revolution reaching into every area of our national life and touching the springs of private thinking. It is a revolution that must begin with us, for the grandeur of a nation and the wisdom of its leaders depend on the moral health of ordinary men and women.

The light that flickers in the White House or in the halls of Congress grows brilliant only as it borrows strength from thoughtful, spiritually dedicated people everywhere. The tide is ours to claim, if we have the strength and the courage.

A Word for Honesty

While visiting with a group of educators in a foreign nation, a traveler emphasized the importance of honesty in dealing with people. The educators were mystified. What is honesty? they wanted to know. They seemed to have no word of their own into which they could translate the concept. When it was suggested that honesty is a source of trust and a way of dealing with others on the basis of mutual confidence, they responded, "But we do not trust one another."

To be honest is to be characterized by integrity and straightforwardness in conduct, thought, and speech. It is to be without deceit. Where there is no word for honesty, it is difficult to do business or to establish trust. Promises are not kept, and under-the-table deals are the rule. Doing business with a dishonest man is a hazardous enterprise.

Honesty is an indispensable ingredient in a viable society; otherwise, the whole institution of credit, which conditions not only economic life but every other species of human cooperation, is dissolved. Credibility gaps in politics or business undermine the trust that sustains our common life together.

The word *honesty* is part of our Puritan inheritance, but our habits and dispositions have become something less than Puritan. Shoplifting has become a fine art, and moral opportunism has become the mark of political life. Our "honesty" is shot through with unconscious or conscious reservations that allow us to misrepresent or deceive when the occasion seems to demand application of the reservations.

When Dwight Morrow was running for political office, he remarked, "I refuse to say anything of which I shall be ashamed

127

twenty years from now." His candor was refreshing. He refused to make promises he knew he could not keep or to woo votes with rosy predictions that could not bear the weight of examination. The word *honesty* was part of his vocabulary, but it also was characteristic of his life.

When the time for political elections comes, it would be refreshing to have politicians saying only things of which they would not be ashamed twenty years later. I suspect that candor and grim honesty just might be the key to election. Playing politics with all of the cards on the table may not seem like good politics, but it would be good for the nation. In the long run, it might be good politics as well.

Benjamin Franklin noted that "truth and sincerity have a certain distinguishing native luster about them which cannot be perfectly counterfeited; they are like fire and flame that cannot be painted." The "distinguishing native luster," however, has compelling force that can be translated into trust. Sooner or later deceptions betray themselves.

The young often tell us they cannot trust what they call the "establishment." They say they find in us too many credibility gaps and a vast difference between what we say and what we do. They accuse us of being essentially dishonest and hypocritical. No doubt they have a point, namely, that we have undermined their faith in us and in the system we have created.

It may be that the decline of spiritual concern in our secular world has weakened our ethical fiber. As Voltaire noted, "When there is no God, all is permitted." When we cease to worship, we cease to care deeply for ethical values. William Ernest Hocking, the philosopher, summarized what religion is trying to do in and through individuals. He wrote: "Only religion can create the unpurchasable man. And it is only the man unpurchasable by society who can create a sound society. And the society of unpurchasable men, with a moral anchor outside their own national life, is the only society that can beget world unity." Only a society of unpurchasable men, whose honesty is transparent, can create the trust that is necessary to sustain society.

At Ease in Sincerity

A familiar sight in my boyhood was the peddler's wagon. The seedy-looking horse stood patiently brushing flies from his flanks with his long tail while neighborhood customers viewed the varied and sundry items of the wagon's stock. The peddler's coming always occasioned considerable excitement during the summer months when school was out, and we youngsters inspected the wares displayed. When we were around, the peddler always seemed a little uneasy, as if we might be disposed to deviltry of one sort or another.

My father always took a dim view of the peddlers. The suspicion that cheap and adulterated goods were presented as the finest and the best lurked in his mind. He did not suggest that the peddlers were deliberately dishonest, but he tended to believe they were not entirely trustworthy. They were inclined, my father thought, to "gild the lily" to make sales.

All of us, I suspect, are guilty of the peddler's disease. We "gild the lily" in our conversations. Our sales pitch may omit mention of the small print. Our gossip may be tinged with exaggeration. A story in the Talmud illustrates the truth. It concerns a king with two jesters whose wise humor was the talk of the kingdom. One day, the king sent them on an errand. "Simon, my fool," he said, "go out and bring back the best thing in the world; and you, John, go out and secure for me the worst thing in the world."

In a short time, the two clowns were back. Simon bowed low and said, "The best thing in the world, sire!" The opened package revealed a tongue. John began to laugh and, quickly unwrapping his bundle, said, "The worst thing in the world, O King," and behold another tongue.

129

Speech, of course, is one of man's greatest gifts and, at the same time, offers his most dangerous capacity. The tongue of a Socrates, speaking from the heart, or the tongue of an Isaiah or an Albert Schweitzer, all practical proponents of their convictions, was responsible for endless good. On the other hand, the tongue of an Adolf Hitler or a Joseph Stalin, speaking deceit and hatred, was capable of devastating wrong. Ecclesiastes estimated that "more have fallen before the tongue than before the sword."

We have a way of selling out to the expedient, saying what we do not mean in order to accommodate ourselves to the feelings of those around us or for the sake of our own interests. I dare say there are many television entertainers promoting products in which they do not believe. On the other hand, there are entertainers like Stan Freberg, offbeat comedian, who are strictly honest. Freberg has refused to perform in Las Vegas. "I am opposed to that city on moral grounds," he said. A successful maker of commercials, he refuses to promote a product he cannot support. So he takes neither tobacco nor liquor advertising.

We cannot afford the peddler's temptation to engage in deception if we expect to be trusted. Albert Camus, in speaking of a friend, remarked, "He is at ease in sincerity." Then he added a postscript: "very rare." However rare it is to be "at ease in sincerity," it is the cornerstone of creative human relationships.

Wise Men Fish Here

A weather-beaten sign outside a New York City bookstore proclaims, Wise Men Fish Here. Inside the store, thoughtful men and women browse and buy. The well-stocked shelves and counters offer books designed for the taste of discriminating readers. New books and priceless first editions of old books abound.

Viewing the bookstore sign from the outside, one may wonder if we are doing enough fishing in good books to inspire wisdom. Few care to grapple with the ideas of Plato, John Dewey, Augustine, or William James while football gladiators provide television entertainment. Digging into the past in quest of historical perspective to frame our understanding of contemporary events requires intellectual discipline for which we have little taste.

Wisdom for the living of these days, however, does not emerge in casual fashion. It is a painstaking search requiring much reading and hard thinking. A philosophy of life to keep us steady through good times and bad emerges only as we brood over the great thoughts of intellectual and spiritual pioneers and prophets. Faith to live by grows, not in a vacuum, but in a mind nurtured and inspired by the spiritual giants of the past.

It is suggestive to notice that Abraham Lincoln's schooling was negligible, the aggregate, he said, not amounting to one year. The boy, however, had access to a few books. He dug into them in such fashion that they left a permanent mark on his mind. The evidence of his deep reading is to be found in the elegance of his style and the richness of his thought.

Lincoln tells us that the books he mastered were the Bible, *Aesop's Fables,* the *Autobiography of Benjamin Franklin,* Shakespeare's plays, Daniel Defoe's *Robinson Crusoe,* John Bunyan's

Pilgrim's Progress, and Mason Locke Weems' *Life of Washington.* Lincoln's mastery of these books gave his mind a solid base for the creative thinking and the clear philosophy of his later years.

Our reading choices are far more varied than those of Lincoln, whose early life was circumscribed by poverty and very limited avenues of culture. As for us, the best thinking of the world is available for the asking in libraries and in bookstores. We may fish in whatever intellectual waters we wish, shallow or deep. Whatever we may say of Lincoln's reading fare, it was neither shallow nor trivial.

We would do well to fish in deep waters. It is only as we launch out into the deep, over our heads perhaps, that our minds are challenged. The Bible still warrants more attention than it receives, offering both a philosophy and a faith for those willing to seek until they find. Shakespeare is by no means a back number, even though he has fallen slightly out of vogue. Ben Franklin still has something to say to our time.

In the long run, it isn't the number of books we read, but the quality, that matters. William Ernest Hocking, the distinguished philosopher, used to say that an educated man ought to have in his mind what he called "a map of the ages," a sense of the flow of history and the ideas that have motivated mankind. Alfred North Whitehead suggested the need for what he called "the habitual vision of greatness" to stimulate and motivate great living. Arnold Toynbee in *A Study of History* has provided "a map of the ages" for us, and a multitude of excellent biographies offer "the habitual vision of greatness." Perspective, insight, challenge, and understanding are ours if we are willing to admit the good sense of the bookstore sign: Wise Men Fish Here.

Few would deny that at such a time as this we need all the wisdom and stability we can find. Ignorance is no virtue in a world at the crossroads. What we need is wisdom for the road ahead and faith to sustain us through the anguish of the present. Both are to be found if we fish in deep waters.

The Family Isn't Finished

Recently I read an article on the theme, "The Family Is Finished." It left me feeling happily old-fashioned and contentedly out of date. The author extolled the delights of freedom in the new permissive world in which men and women enjoy each other without family responsibility or marital ties that bind. Why should anyone want to be tied down to one partner when many are available and variety is the spice of life?

It was the assumption of the article that most couples embarking on a traditional marriage are undertaking an assignment beyond their capacities. The ideals of conventional marriage are so unrealistic they won't hold water. The repressive rules and regulations binding two people together "until death do us part" do not fit present society.

So, if traditional marriage is out and permissive freedom is in, the family is finished. The new freedom, unencumbered by rules or discipline, makes life fun and thoroughly pleasurable. Who wants the burden of a family when we can be free to do as we please? Diapers and snuggle bunnies are out, and baby food is for the birds.

In my perversely out-of-date way, I started thinking about the fun and satisfactions the freedom cult is missing. There is the wonder of watching youngsters grow, testing their minds and their muscles; the happy banter and camaraderie of the dinner table; and the fellowship of fishing, swimming, and playing baseball together. There are those moments when confidences are shared and love is revealed. They are priceless.

It isn't all roses, of course, but permissiveness, too, has its pains. Jens Peter Jacobsen suggests the hazards of hedonism in his novel,

Niels Lyhns. In the story, Erich, in his relationship with Fenni-more, "lacked the fine ... tenderness that protects the loved woman against herself and watches over her dignity." And Fenni-more "did not know that the intoxication which uplifts takes its strength from the wings of tomorrow" and in the end becomes "utterly bitter."

If we could stay always young, we might face the new freedom with greater confidence. The years, however, bring a new dimension to our thinking. We become aware of our need for relationships that last, for the warmth of home and family, and for memories to enrich the days and nights. Children and grandchildren bring an inner satisfaction that is hard to match.

Eugene O'Neill in *Ah, Wilderness,* for all his cynicism, caught something of the meaning of permanence in relationships. In one scene, Richard quotes *The Rubáiyát* to his wife:

Ah, that Spring should vanish with the Rose!
That Youth's sweet-scented manuscript should close!

And he adds: "Well, Spring isn't everything, is it, Essie? There's a lot to be said for Autumn. That's got beauty, too. And Winter—if you're together."

Yes, even winter has its compensations if we are together, surrounded by children and grandchildren. There is a warmth and glow to life, a sense of fulfillment and meaning in the sunset years if we have built on solid ground in the spring of life.

The simple truth is that disciplined years of youth and spring bring satisfying years of autumn and winter. Profligate years of spring turn out to be bitter in winter. The new freedom may seem pleasant for a while, but it leads to disillusionment. Discipline imposes limits on our freedom, but it results finally in a greater freedom to achieve and to find meaning in life.

When Silence Is Wisdom

After a particularly vitriolic and dissension-filled faculty meeting, a professor remarked that he had found it difficult not to give some of his colleagues a piece of his mind. "Fortunately," he said, "I have learned that what I don't say, I don't have to regret."

Now and then, when we are disturbed, if not infuriated, by the nitwit opinions of the loquacious, it is good to remember the comment of Jonathan Swift in *Gulliver's Travels*. He wrote, "There are times when talk is hurtful and when silence is the beginning of wisdom." Then he asked bluntly, "Do you know when?" Too often, I suspect, most of us speak when we ought to keep still and keep silent when we ought to speak out.

There are times when it is necessary for us quietly to affirm our convictions. Frequently, however, when we are saying something rather significant, we say it with an overabundance of authority. We argue vigorously over matters that haven't the slightest importance. Red in the face, we make outrageous statements that in retrospect we regret. At such times, we would do well to remember the advice of Paul, the apostle, given to his young friend, Timothy, "Be ambitious to be quiet."

An American League baseball manager once noted the way Charles Berry, a wise, one-time umpire, often dealt with angry managers and players. Berry had a way of letting a man talk himself out. "He holds off," a manager said, in some irritation, "and makes a man exaggerate his claims. Then the man gets to feeling he's being ridiculous and shuts his mouth."

One able business leader, who has been of great service not only to his particular field but to the civic interests of the nation and the world, told Lowell Ditzen that from time to time he requested his secretary to bring in a little typewritten card for him to read at the beginning of the day. It had these words on it: Have you asked God to help you keep your big mouth shut today?

Silence is the essence of wisdom, especially when personalities become involved in discussions. Saying nasty things about other people leaves us with mud on our own faces. Denunciation changes nothing. It only serves to increase hostility, and, as William Cowper wrote in "The Task":

> Disgust concealed
> Is ofttimes proof of wisdom, when the fault
> Is obstinate, and the cure beyond our reach.

Political discussion frequently becomes acrimonious, punctuated by a minimum of thought. Solos and monologues come to be prolonged and repetitive, evidence of strong feeling without reason or logic. We would be wise to speak with quiet clarity, listen with dignity, and brood methodically in quest of insight and understanding. The hard issues of our time will not yield to loud speaking.

At another time of political contest, Thomas Carlyle wrote a letter to Ralph Waldo Emerson that speaks to our need. He wrote: "If I were a legislator, I would order every man, once a week or so, to lock his lips together, and utter no vocable at all for four-and-twenty hours: it would do him an immense benefit, poor fellow. Such racket, and cackle of mere hearsay and sincere-cant grows at last entirely deafening, enough to drive one mad—like the voice of mere infinite rookeries answering your voice! Silence, Silence!"

There is a business executive I greatly admire. Again and again I have watched him at meetings listening in silence to the arguments, following the conversation thoughtfully. Then, when time for decision arrives, he summarizes the arguments of those participating in the meeting, and, in concise language, suggests what ought to be done. Nine times out of ten, his proposals are adopted because they cut through the verbiage to the question at issue. Listening in silence and thinking, he then speaks with wisdom.

Trail of Tears

A thoughtful friend gave me a paperweight in which is embedded a miniature of a famous painting by Jerome Tiger, a gifted Indian painter who died in 1967. The painting is entitled, *Trail of Tears,* history's name for the tragic removal of American Indians from their homes in the South to raw Indian territory in the 1830s.

In the foreground of Tiger's painting, an Indian brave kneels beside his wife and child in a barren waste of snow. The mother, sitting on an outcropping of rock, clings to her half-dead child, while the cold wind whips her black hair over her face. In the background, a tattered group plods through the snow in helpless despair. The painting suggests both tears and tragedy.

As I studied the painting, my thoughts traveled to the tears of little children I saw in India, their bellies swelled with wind and emptiness; to the haunting agony of a mother in Korea, scrounging for food for her two children after war had ravaged her country; to the sad faces of men and women haunted by poverty in Nepal and Egypt; and to the anguish of refugees in the camps of Lebanon and Syria.

The "Trail of Tears" is not an isolated event in history, but a tragic reality for millions throughout the earth. Hunger and fear stalk the world, and the bitterness of the dispossessed chills the cultural landscape. Hostility and anger lurk close to the tears, and resentment strikes out in fruitless violence.

Once, when the world was large and empty spaces vast, it was easier to ignore the tears and the hurts of the many too many. We could bask in our own comfort and security and let the rest of the world go by. But now, with the world shrunk to a neighborhood by commerce and communication, technology and tele-

137

vision, what happens anywhere has repercussions everywhere.

There always are those waiting in the wings, eager to exploit tears and anguish for their own ends. They come with seductive promises of Utopia when they take command of things. They wait patiently, cultivating resentment and bitterness, until they are able to strike and move into some vacuum of power. If they leave a "Trail of Tears" in their wake, a trail more agonizing than the one before, they could not care less.

A farmer in India, eeking out a precarious living on a little plot of land, listened to the paeans of praise heaped on the Communist giant to the north, and wondered, What do I have to lose? Freedom has no meaning when there is neither dignity nor bread for life. Liberty is a chimera when there is no hope. On the "Trail of Tears," values and ideals lose their grip on the minds and hearts of men and women.

It is ironic that we must spend billions for defense while more and more of the hungry undermine our security, turning in desperation and despair to pseudo-saviors. More and more, we find ourselves alone, an oasis of plenty in a world of want and tears. Much of the world would starve without the bounty of the wheat fields of Kansas, Texas, Oklahoma, Colorado, and the Dakotas. But hunger and tears persist.

No nation has been more generous with its bounty than we or more disposed to share our knowledge and technology with the rest of the world. Unhappily, overpopulation, ignorance, superstition, and conflict have thwarted progress in the Third World and made it incredibly difficult for the people to help themselves. As on a treadmill, they continue to travel on the "Trail of Tears."

Should we, then, retreat into fortress America and let the rest of the world go by? Or, despite criticism and rejection, should we go on doing what we are able to alleviate hunger and want in the world? The answer, of course, is the humane one. Recently, the churches of the nation asked their members to sacrifice a major meal a week and give to a fund for hunger not only to help feed the hungry but also to make each of us aware that our plenty should be shared with those in need.

Our own destiny is linked inextricably with those who travel the "Trail of Tears." If our response is one of aloofness and indifference, theirs will be one of hostility and anger. Our compassion and helpfulness can yield a benediction of hope.

Who Cares?

There is no cry of the human spirit more poignant than the one that came from the lips of the author of Psalm 142, "No man cares for me." It is a cry of loneliness, isolation, and alienation. William Cowper phrased the same feelings in "Verses":

> I am out of humanity's reach,
> I must finish my journey alone,
> Never hear the sweet music of speech;
> I start at the sound of my own.

Such feelings, unfortunately, are all too common. The aged, whose active years have ended, often wonder, Who cares? Once, they were somebodies; now, they feel like nobodies. Their children, preoccupied with their own families, have little time for them. Theirs is often a sense of the uselessness suggested in "Growing Old" by Karle Wilson Baker:

> The poor scarecrow stands
> Lonely and old and useless;
> The last crow has gone.

Strangely enough, it is not just the aged who wonder, Who cares? The haunting question comes to most of us at one time or another. The teenager, alienated from his parents, feeling misunderstood and perhaps unwanted, travels a lonely road. His yearning for affection and love is deeper than words can tell. He may at times seem unapproachable and hostile, but even these attitudes are reflections of his inner pain.

Women often feel a letdown after their children have gone to college or have been married; troubled by feelings of no longer being needed, they wonder if anybody cares anymore. Men passed over in the business-promotion scramble may also feel neglected and resentful. They ask themselves, Doesn't anyone appreciate the months and years they gave to their company? Who cares, now that their best years are gone?

It isn't surprising that in the absence of love and caring, many turn to drink and drugs. It becomes their way, as someone suggested, of "spitting in fate's eye." They feel the kind of frustration expressed by T. S. Eliot in *The Cocktail Party:*

> There was a door
> And I could not open it. I could not touch the handle.

To Eliot, it is a state of hell because "hell is alone."

With so many people crying out for friendship, love, and appreciation, it is curious that we give so little of these ingredients of a full life to others. Could it be that we are afraid to reveal our feelings for fear of rejection? Do we fail to say "I love you" because we are uncomfortable with what we think may be sentimentality? Or are we so preoccupied with ourselves and with our own personal needs that we overlook the universal need to express affection and love?

Jurgen Moltmann, a distinguished theologian, notes that "only in his outgoing towards the world does man experience himself." It is the outgoingness that is important, the reaching out toward others with goodwill and affection. We experience ourselves at our best in offering affection and love, appreciation and concern.

It costs very little to offer encouragement to the young who are trying to find themselves, to show some signs of caring to the old who feel lonely and unneeded. But the rewards are great: both young and old respond with joy to even small tokens of concern.

Furthermore, in loving and caring for each other, we come as close to God as man can come. Instead of a remote, awesome deity, God then becomes as close to us as the affection we share, the love we express, and the caring we show. He is wherever friendship is growing and love is healing hidden hurts. He is where sympathy sheds a tear or kindness lifts the burden of disappointment.

Fit to Be Wanted

One of the hazards of old age is the disposition to fall into the not-wanted syndrome. It is all too easy for us to feel unwanted and not needed, as if life had passed us by without much notice. There are those who nourish their self-pity and walk about all draped in reeds, like a weeping willow tree. They feel resentful and sometimes bitter at being neglected.

Many years ago, I preached a sermon on the theme, "Fit to Be Wanted." It was not a sermon on old age, but the more I have thought about the matter, the more I have been convinced that the major business of old age is to be fit to be wanted. If we find ourselves bitter and resentful, we really are not fit to be wanted anywhere. In *Romeo and Juliet,* one character says to another, "Thy head is as full of quarrels as an egg is full of meat." If that description fits, we are not likely to be wanted.

There is a striking story about an elderly lady, opinionated and quarrelsome, who frequently visited her married daughter on weekends. Her son-in-law was in the navy and was incapacitated now and then by outbreaks of the hives. After some months of treatment, a dermatologist discovered that the hives always developed the day following the visit of the mother-in-law. To say that the mother-in-law was not wanted would be an understatement. So far as our children are concerned, the ultimate advice to us oldsters should be, Always remember you are a guest.

Part of the problem of being not fit to be wanted is in the fact age is tempted to be more self-concerned than other-concerned. We have a tendency to remind people that in "the good old days" we were somebodies and to regale others with recitals of our achievements. Unfortunately, people just are not interested in the recitals of those Archie Bunker described as hold-overs

141

and has-beens. People would prefer that we be interested in them.

We alienate our young ones, too, when we are disposed to give too much good advice. They do not want it, thank you, unless they ask for it. Incidentally, they are more likely to ask for it if we do not offer it gratuitously. François de La Rochefoucauld observed pertinently that "old people delight in giving good advice because they no longer can set bad examples."

Then, too, as we grow older, our opinions tend to become crystallized. We have decided opinions. But, as Herbert Prochnow commented, "In an elder statesman wisdom may come with age, but sometimes age comes alone." It comes alone when we are without flexibility, that is, the capacity to revise judgments and take a second look at the things we have taken for granted.

A thoughtful youngster remarked not long ago, "My grandfather knows so much that isn't so." That is a hazard for us oldsters if we are not wise enough to keep open minds and a willingness to consider opinions at variance with our own. The glory of Oliver Wendell Holmes was in the fact that even at eighty he still was appropriating new truth, venturing into new fields of learning. Albert Einstein, still open-minded during his declining years, noted, "I always try to keep the door open a little to peek behind the curtain." Keeping the door open to peek behind the curtain is an important virtue for those of us who are tempted to settle down in our opinions.

If we keep ourselves in perspective, avoid the not-wanted syndrome, and keep the door open for new insights, we will be wanted, despite our faltering steps, our forgetfulness, and all the other limitations of old age. Karle Wilson Baker put the matter wisely in "Growing Old":

> Let me grow lovely, growing old—
> So many fine things do:
> Laces, and ivory, and gold,
> And silk need not be new;
>
> And there is healing in old trees,
> Old streets a glamour hold;
> Why may not I, as well as these,
> Grow lovely, growing old?

Well, why not, if we wish to be fit to be wanted and welcome?

Wisdom for Our Time

Show me his friends and I the man shall know;
This wiser turn a larger wisdom lends:
Show me the books he loves and I shall know
The man far better than through mortal friends.

"Books and the Man" by SILAS WEIR MITCHELL

On Being Too Helpful

Some years ago, a young man, recently married, stopped one evening at his parents' home. His mother, wanting to be wise in dealing with her new daughter-in-law, confronted him with the question, "How am I doing as a mother-in-law?" The question brought an instant response, "Just fine, just fine, mother. Just don't try to be too helpful."

Parents often get into trouble with the wives or husbands of their children simply by trying to be too helpful. Their intentions are good, and yet the newly married couple needs time to work things out together. Being too helpful can frustrate the efforts of young married people to manage their own affairs. They may view the efforts of parents to help as an affront to their own capacity to cope with their new situation.

Most parents, who spend years guiding their youngsters toward maturity, find it difficult to understand that the children no longer need or want their advice. If they do want advice or help they will ask for it. They may not wish to have dinner every Sunday with the folks. They have no desire to report to their parents daily by telephone. They want to be free.

There are times, unfortunately, when parents hang on to their offspring from a sense of their own need. They want to be helpful because they wish to be needed. But, as T. S. Eliot noted in another connection:

> The last temptation is the greatest treason:
> To do the right deed for the wrong reason.

Trying to be too helpful to our children in order to satisfy our own need to be needed is to succumb to the temptation to do what may be the right thing for the wong reason.

Voltaire noted in *Candide* that the ultimate purpose of life is the cultivation of one's own garden. We parents would be wise to remember our married children have a right to cultivate their own garden without interference. They probably will make mistakes as we did when we were young, but they would like to make their own mistakes and to learn from them. They grow in their understanding of each other and of life as they view their mistakes together.

Counseling with young married couples through the years, I am persuaded that the best thing we parents can do is to retire gracefully to tending our own gardens. The more willing we are to retire the more willing they are to invite us to share their lives. When they know we have no desire to interfere or meddle, they welcome us into their ventures. They want us to share the love of their children.

Now and then, things can go wrong even when we parents are trying not to be too helpful. Times of emotional or physical stress can result in thoughtless comments that bruise and hurt. At such times, we need the wisdom of Abraham Lincoln who was confronted by an irritating and cantankerous Edwin Stanton at a cabinet meeting. Stanton wanted Lincoln to blow up, and so he called him a fool. Lincoln, as the famous story goes, never "heard" the word *fool*. He saved face by not hearing it, and this so disconcerted Stanton that he gave in when Lincoln remarked innocuously, "Stanton is usually right."

It isn't always easy to be mothers-in-law or fathers-in-law. There can be heartaches and hurts, but there always are compensating joys and satisfactions, if we consider the positives and minimize the negatives. If we are emotionally mature, we will so love our young ones that we refuse to smother them but set them free to fulfill the promise of their lives. We will love their children without trying to possess them.

There was gentle wisdom in the comment, "Just don't try to be too helpful." We can be open and receptive without prying; thoughtful and considerate without interfering; loving and affectionate without being demanding. Love and understanding between us and our married children can mature into a delightful fellowship that will be a benediction to them and to us.

No Philosophy; No Rules

The word *philosophy* originally meant "the love of wisdom or knowledge." It has come to mean "a particular system of principles and laws for the conduct of life." Philosophy defines our values and our goals and purposes. It gives a sense of direction and meaning to the struggles of our days.

Every society, from the most primitive to the most advanced, has depended for its survival on some system of principles and laws for the conduct of life. Ancient Greece and Rome had their gods who imposed standards of conduct on their devotees. Both nations decayed when their gods were discredited. Inevitably, when rules and laws, undergirded by religious faith, are undermined, the result is disintegration.

The meaning of Lynette ("Squeaky") Fromme, who tried to assassinate President Ford, is implicit in her observation that "if you have no philosophy, you don't have any rules." Essentially, if we have no philosophy, we can do as we please. There simply are no rules or laws to guide conduct and no rule worth preserving. Love and licentiousness are equally good; cheating and honesty are interchangeable. One is no better than the other.

"Squeaky" Fromme is the ultimate illustration of permissiveness devoid of philosophy. Words like *sin* and *evil* are relics of Victorian intolerance. Distinctions between right and wrong are merely semantic, without reference to any objective standards of behavior. God is dead, and the Judeo-Christian ethic is merely a hangover from an archaic past.

It is true, of course, that no era of history has been devoid of wrong, evil, sin, and corruption. Unlike the present, however, the past had a philosophy grounded in religious faith that made

147

distinctions between right and wrong, good and evil. Our Puritan past may have been overly intolerant and inflexible, but at least it had a system of principles and values for the guidance of behavior.

"Squeaky" Fromme may be an amoral freak, without principles or a sense of values, but she illustrates the ethical climate of society as do those industrial executives guilty of bribery and unlawful political contributions. Scandals of one sort or another are making the headlines of newspapers too frequently to be ignored. They range from doctors cheating welfare patients and the government to lawyers with their reputations tarnished in the Watergate affair.

The social fabric is a fragile thing, hung together by ideals and values, principles and standards, cherished by individuals. Every deviation from honorable standards of behavior weakens the social fabric, tears it ever so little, making it less strong. Each violation of trust shreds the common fabric of trust and lessens our confidence in each other. So, in a very real sense, what happens anywhere, happens everywhere.

When we have no philosophy and anything goes, the fibers that hold society together are weakened beyond repair. Outworn traditions of chivalry become moribund, and womanhood is degraded. Old-fashioned notions of honesty and industry become musty with disuse and the marts of trade cease to flourish. Without principles and laws, society blunders toward anarchy.

When we have no philosophy to guide us, a philosophy anchored in God, we are cut adrift in an unfriendly sea. We have no compass to guide us to harbor, no stars to point the way of our going. So we drift with the tide, doing what others, equally lost, are doing. We have no way of knowing what is ethical and what is unethical, what is right and what is wrong.

Nobody yet has improved on the Ten Commandments and the Beatitudes as valid guides for conduct. They offer principles and laws that are sound, not because they are reputed to have come from God on Mount Sinai or because Jesus uttered them, but because they are viable and true in human experience. They represent the distilled wisdom of the ages coined into the wisdom of God. It is time we staked our philosophy, our faith, and our lives on their time-tested moral guidance.

Going Too Fast

Sir William Osler, one-time Regius professor of medicine at the University of Oxford, told members of a graduating class that they should cultivate "coolness and presence of mind under all circumstances, calmness amid storms, clearness of judgment in moments of great peril." The advice has merit, not only for doctors, but for all of us.

Capacity to make sound judgments and to preserve "coolness and presence of mind" requires both time and reflection. It is not acquired without habits of quiet thought tempering the hurried pace of our ordinary days. "Slow me down, Lord, I'm going too fast" is a message we all need if we are to achieve the maturity of mind and spirit suggested by Dr. Osler.

Ours might well be called the age of the immediate. We want instant results, instant judgment, and instant maturity along with our instant coffee. But the mills of wisdom grind slowly, and we mature only as we meditate on the meaning of our experiences.

Unfortunately, the present always is present, its problems and issues urgent. We can't seem to escape from the immediate and the necessary. The result is that we seldom find time to consider long-range goals that could give meaning to our lives. An article by Dennis Farney, entitled "Rocky's Harassed Think Tank," suggested that the problem of the White House Domestic Council is the fact that "short-range problems are forever crowding out long-range problems." There isn't time to consider the future because of immediate pressures.

The nation, like individuals, requires thinking to define goals and rearrange priorities. Unhappily, Washington has all too little time for thinking. By going too fast, we become like two pre-

149

historic characters strolling through the cartoon strip "B. C." One character says to the other, "Where are we going?" The answer, "Nowhere." The response, "I have a question. . . . Why are we going so fast?" That is a question we need to ask ourselves.

There are times when we go farther because our pace is more measured. We go in the direction of our goals and with distinct purpose when we are thinking as we go, moving only when we know where we are going and why. We stop burning energy going around in circles at a furious pace and make our steps count. Speed sometimes creates the illusion of command, but, without reflection, it leaves us and our world as before.

When we say we do not have time for reflection, we delude ourselves. We find time for whatever we consider to be important. Reflection and meditation are as important to the life of the mind and to sound judgment as exercise is to the body. They are necessary if we are to achieve "coolness and presence of mind under all circumstances."

The Lincolns and the Churchills show the strength of reflective minds. They stood out above the crowds in times of peril as men of judgment and wisdom, enduring criticism and difficulty with equanimity. Lincoln's reflection led him to the discovery of spiritual values and resources that kept him steady under the vast pressures of his office during the Civil War. As he put it, "Amid the greatest difficulties of my administration, when I could not see any other resort, I would place my whole reliance in God."

We deal wisely and competently with the issues of the immediate when our reflection and meditation have led to the discovery of what someone called "the Beyond that is within." When we are going too fast, we miss the priceless ingredients of stability and wisdom that give direction to our movement.

Moral Balance

Some time ago, I was surprised to see a friend of mine devastatingly drunk at a convention in New York City. I knew him as a respectable and upright citizen of good habits in Chicago, where he lived. But, obviously, his ways of behaving away from home were quite different from his circumspect conduct when he was on home grounds.

My friend was an illustration of the comment of William Lyon Phelps: "There are some people who are all right at 3 o'clock in the afternoon, but watch out for them at 3 o'clock in the morning. They are all right in Yonkers, but look out for them in Paris. They are all right when they associate with virtuous people, but look out for them when they associate with evil companions."

The trouble is that some of us are weak at the center, at the mercy of time and place. When in Rome, we do as the Romans do, but we are not masters of ourselves. We run with the tide, but we seldom go against it. We are pushed around by the company we keep because we have no great convictions to hold us to a steady course. We bounce along with whatever wind happens to be blowing at the moment.

There isn't much strain on a man's character when he is in a prayer meeting. But when he kisses his wife good-bye and boards a train or a plane for a convention in another city, the strain becomes acute. The customs and inhibitions that surround him in the local community where he catches the 8:05 train each morning vanish, and he is on his own. He is stuck with only the moral and spiritual resources he brought along inside himself. Too often when he gets to Paris, or wherever he's headed, he's just "gone with the wind."

When a group of high school parents got together a little while ago, the discussion centered on the question: How can we get our boys to the point where they will be able to keep their moral balance when they get into college? It is a difficult question. How does any man or woman stand up under moral strain when the tides are running against everything for which he or she should stand, everything he or she believes in?

Part of the answer goes back to deeply rooted convictions about life's meaning and destiny. A young woman put the truth bluntly when she came into my study. She was a most attractive person who had come to the city from a small town. When she sat down, she seemed slightly belligerent, and she startled me with her first question. "Can you tell me any good reason why I shouldn't have an affair with a married man in the office where I work?" she asked. "Well," I responded. "What's holding you back? Why did you come to see me?" She burst into tears and answered, "Everything I ever believed or thought is holding me back." Then she choked back her tears and went on, "But he says I'm just a relic of the Victorian era."

The truth of the matter is plain enough. We are held steady under strain at 3 A.M. in Yonkers or in Paris, in good company or in bad, by what we believe most deeply. If we believe that honor is worth keeping at any cost, we will cling to honor under stress. If we believe deeply that a man ought to be a gentleman at home or abroad because it is right to be a gentleman, we will stand steady when the tide is pulling at our feet.

Essentially, we need to start where Robert Louis Stevenson started when he said, "I believe in the ultimate decency of things, and if I wake up in hell I will still believe in it." Of course, Stevenson believed in "the essential decency of things" because he believed in God. So, when the tides were against decency and honor and integrity, he could stand by them in Yonkers or in Paris at 3:00 o'clock in the afternoon or at 3:00 o'clock in the morning, unshakable in his inner strength.

Keeping our moral balance in Paris, in college, in the army, or at a convention is mostly a matter of believing profoundly in "the essential decency of things" because we believe in God.

Stoplights

We live in a society afflicted with stoplights. The other day, when I was in a hurry to get somewhere, the green lights turned to red every time I came to an intersection. I had to stop and wait, frustrated by red lights that inhibited my progress. There was nothing I could do about it.

My blood pressure built up every time a red light stopped me in my tracks. I wanted to get to where I was going, and to get there on time. I should have started sooner, but I hadn't, so I fumed at the lights as if someone had put them there to frustrate me personally. When I got to thinking about the matter, I felt more than a little foolish.

Life is largely a matter of coping with stoplights. We set out to accomplish something we think is worthwhile, and, before we are well on our way, we run into a red light. Not long ago, a man said, "Everything was going beautifully and then my heart kicked up. Now the future looks grim." A troubled woman said sadly, "We thought things were going well for our family, and we just got word that Billy has flunked out of college."

Stoplights are beyond our control, and we have no choice but to deal with them sensibly. That seemed clear one night coming into O'Hare airport in Chicago in a fog. The pilot announced it would be forty-five minutes before we could land. When we finally landed, the pilot announced we would have to wait for an open ramp to disembark. We sat on the field for another thirty minutes.

It was interesting to watch the passengers. Some were grumbling over the delay; others were fuming because they would miss connections; still others were arguing with the stewardesses.

Through it all, a woman across the aisle was quietly reading a book. She seemed completely at ease and unconcerned by the delay. When we finally got up to leave the plane, she remarked, "Well, I've missed my plane to Kansas City. I hope there is another one tonight." Obviously, she had learned to cope with stoplights she could not control. Her plans had been upset, but she was serene.

Two things can be said about the way we deal with red lights that thwart us. The first is that we can see them as a challenge to self-control and self-discipline. A teacher, Annie Keary, once wrote to a girl who, because of circumstances she could not control, had to leave school. "I think I find most help," Miss Keary wrote, "in trying to look on all interruptions and hindrances . . . as discipline, trials . . . to help one against getting selfish." Fussing, fuming, and tension because of stoplights are evidences of selfishness, not self-control. When we want things to go our way, the fog to clear, and ramps to be open to suit our convenience, the frustrations that result can be a challenge to recognize our selfishness and find inner serenity.

The second observation is that the way we deal with stoplights is evidence of the significance of our faith. The quality of faith is revealed in the way we cope with what we cannot avoid. I know nothing about the lady reading a book across the aisle while we were trying to land at O'Hare Field, but I dare say she was a woman of quiet faith, a faith that enabled her to meet the unavoidable with serenity.

On Talking Too Much

It was Louis Armstrong who remarked, "You can say what you like on the slide trombone, but you gotta be careful with words." Unfortunately, we are not as careful with words as we should be. We speak before we think and then wish we had kept still. We reveal confidences we had promised to keep, and we indulge in aimless chatter that goes nowhere.

Despite the plethora of words, we seem unable to get through to each other. Tom Lehrer, the singing humorist, remarks in one of his songs that nowadays everybody is complaining that they can't communicate. Parents say they are unable to communicate with their children and vice versa. Husbands say they cannot communicate with their wives, and wives are depressed because they cannot communicate with their husbands. Lehrer concludes humorously that if we can't communicate, the least we can do is to shut up.

Certainly, there are times when "silence is golden," and we communicate more adequately and helpfully when we keep still long enough to think before we allow our tongues to wag. The unstoppable monologue, with unrelated ideas strung together with "ahs," thwarts the possibility of communication. The floor is preempted, and the exchange of thoughts is stifled by the equivalent of a filibuster.

A middle-aged woman, accustomed to talking most of the time, often about the sins and foibles of others, responded to a rebuke by saying, "I am not a gossip, so help me God! I am gossiped to and I only repeat what I have heard from others." There ought to be, I am persuaded, an inalienable right not to listen, to shut out inane monologues and unsavory gossip.

In the Scriptures, James notes that "the tongue is a little member, and boasts of great things. How great a forest is set ablaze by a small fire. And the tongue is a fire." That is a refined way of saying "you gotta be careful with words." They can cause no end of trouble. The gossip leaves a trail of misery in his wake. The hostile tongue sets fires of resentment and anger. The sharp tongue of supposed superiority invites retaliation.

There are times when it seems as if the tongue were a source, not of communication, but of noncommunication. Words divide us into warring camps, and we talk past each other rather than to each other. In anger, we say what we do not mean and, to our sorrow, we cannot recall the words we have spoken. We inflict wounds on each other with words that are sharper than swords.

Let there be no mistake, "you gotta be careful with words." They can destroy or they can build. They can inspire confidence or invite despair. They have within them the seeds of joy or the seeds of sadness. Words of encouragement are able to generate great accomplishment; words of criticism can germinate into defeat. The tongue is a little member, but it can boast of great things, either good or evil.

When we are inclined to talk too much, we would be wise to "stop, look, and listen" in order to measure the impact of what we intend to say. In his book *Civilization and Its Discontents*, Sigmund Freud observes that an indispensable characteristic of civilization is the willingness of people not to say and not to do some things they want to say or do. In a sense, we are civilized when we refuse to communicate to others what we ought to keep to ourselves.

The art of creative living hinges on the wisdom to know the difference between what we ought to communicate and what we should keep to ourselves. There are times when silence is wisdom, and there are times when it is not. The retreat into silence and refusal to speak can be an invitation to conflict. A gentle word, spoken with compassion, can be a source of healing and understanding. A brutal word unsaid, restrained in silence, is wise.

The basic truth can be summed up in the comment, "you gotta be careful with words." The tongue can be a fire, and by it a "great forest is set ablaze" with consequences we cannot estimate or control. Only self-control can prevent the fire.

It Isn't Really New

One of the curious things about the "sexplosion" of our time is the assumption that it is something new under the sun. It is fair to say it is new here in the United States where "sexploitation" has become a popular form of conspicuous consumption. We seem to think we are in the vanguard of enlightened new freedom, liberating mankind from the restraints of traditional Puritanism.

The facts of history, however, belie the newness of our liberation. Group sex is as old as the baths of ancient Rome. What is more, ancient Babylon had its nude dancers and its public display of sex. When the first Israelite families settled in Canaan, the fertility cults posed a problem that threatened the moral values of the immigrants. The pornography of Ovid, Sappho, and Catullus was celebrated while the Roman Empire was in the process of disintegration.

If we take time to study the Bible, we discover it includes references to sexual aberrations from sodomy to homosexuality, from mass orgies around a golden calf, to adulteries and the celebrations of sex. The Scriptures are altogether honest about the perversions of the past. One might ask, What's new?

The pill is new. Motion pictures and television are new, and these mass media present pornography on a large scale. They mock the old taboos and encourage a permissive society whose outlines are etched in the increasing nudity and frankness of today's films, in the obscene language of novels, and in the candid lyrics of pop songs. Our liberation from the ethical standards of yesterday has moved with astonishing rapidity.

A young woman facing divorce summed up the truth about our permissive society when she remarked, "We seem to have lost con-

157

trol of our lives." Contemporary cultural standards have undermined our sense of values. There is no consensus on such crucial issues as premarital sex, extramarital sex, birth control, and abortion. We are a generation out of control, thinking we are liberated, when, in reality, we are becoming captives of our permissiveness.

Malcolm Muggeridge, British social commentator, suggested perceptively that, when the arteries of discipline harden, "our vitality ebbs" and "people reach out for vicarious excitement, like the current sex mania in pop songs and popular press." He notes that a similar sex mania preceded the fall of Rome and adds, "There is an analogy here for us."

When we are living in what Max Lerner calls "a Babylonian society, perhaps more Babylonian than Babylon itself," the limits of our self-control are narrowed. When the emphasis in society is on the senses and the release of the sensual, our inhibitions are weakened and, too easily, we become victims of the social climate, not masters of our own destinies.

We seldom know the limits of our self-control and, therefore, we expose ourselves to situations that sweep us off our ethical feet. The adolescent who insists on liberty unlimited on the assumption that he can take care of himself anywhere frequently blunders beyond his depth. He becomes a captive of the sensate, not the master of his life and his choices. His freedom to choose wisely is in jeopardy.

"Sex is dynamite," Joseph Fletcher wrote. "Unchanneled by high character it leads to chaos and destruction. It can be the fiercest cement of relationship, but it also can be the lever that breaks people apart." In a very real sense, sex can be used for better living or for self-destruction. It can be a meaningful, enriching, and creative experience, or it can be personally and socially destructive.

It is worth noting that the newest thing in history is monogamy, with one man living with one woman through thick and thin "until death do us part." Centuries of human experience went into the discovery that both vital personality and social stability require instinctive discipline and self-control and that the family is a necessary ingredient in a viable civilization.

In the days to come, we will have to choose whether we wish to out-Babylon the past or to recover our faith in the ideals and values history has proved valid for personal life and society.

Terminable or Permanent

The assumption of the past that marriage should last "until death do us part" appears to be outmoded in contemporary society. There are many who seem to be proceeding on the premise, "Try it, you might like it, but if not, forget it." As Margaret Mead, the anthropologist, remarked, "The most serious thing that is happening in the United States is that people enter marriage now with the idea that it is terminable."

Obviously, marriage is terminable, and increasingly couples are opting out. When problems emerge, as they always do, the tenacity to grapple with dividing issues and resolve them is lacking. Our permissive society has discounted discipline and those qualities of character that make us willing to struggle for understanding of one another.

Too often, I suspect, marriage leads us into a world for which we are not prepared emotionally or spiritually. In our immaturity, we expect Utopia, only to discover the necessity for adjustment, compromise, and tolerance. When our expectations outrun reality, we are unwilling to reexamine our expectations in the light of the possible. So it is that decided opinions collide in conflict.

When marriage fails, we find all manner of excuses that enable us to escape responsibility. Like Mary in Eugene O'Neill's *Long Day's Journey into Night*, we blame failure vaguely on life. She remarks:

> "None of us can help the things life has done to us. They're done before you realize it, and once they're done they make you do other things until at last everything comes between what you'd like to be, and you've lost your true self forever."

Mary's failure was not her fault, she thought. It was the fault of

159

life. She never was able to view herself honestly and admit, as all of us must, that what life does to us depends on what is in us.

It never is easy for us to view ourselves objectively when we are in conflict. It is much simpler to blame someone else or life or circumstances. Unfortunately, in the fixing of blame outside ourselves, there is no hope. Communication ceases and the gulf that separates two people becomes a yawning chasm with no bridge over it.

If, in the face of conflict, we look upon marriage as terminable, divorce appears to be the simplest answer. It isn't really simple. On the contrary, it is complex and difficult in the extreme, especially if children are involved. It may be necessary if one or the other party is immature, selfish, disloyal, or utterly unwilling to face issues with honesty and decent humility. But in any case, it is devastating.

Counseling with couples in conflict always reveals defensiveness, with each party self-protective, standing in the grandeur of his or her own self-righteousness. If there is the confession, "I suppose I am partly at fault," it ends with "but. . . ." It then goes on with accusations, as if the confessed fault were altogether minor in comparison with the guilt of the other.

Those who are finding marriage difficult should be reminded that the social fabric of the nation and the stability of society hinge on marriage and the family as permanent institutions. Professor Edwin Lemert noted in a Task Force Report on the Juvenile Court that the family "even though badly attenuated or disturbed by conflict . . . continues to be the institution of choice for the socialization of children." He adds that scientifically run children's homes, Russian crèches, or Israeli kibbutz nurseries cannot begin to duplicate the mystique "which nurtures children into stable adults."

If the couple in conflict is willing to concede mutual fault and to face themselves, there is hope. If they are mature enough to accept their own responsibility for the conflict between them, they can find their way into a relationship of understanding. If they still cherish hope that their relationship can be permanent, it probably will be so.

So Much We Don't Know

One evening, when we were reading, my wife looked up from the pages of a magazine to inquire, "What does *syzygy* mean?" "It doesn't mean anything to me," I responded. "It probably is a misprint." "No," she said, "it is in an article by a distinguished author, and it must mean something."

"The word has quotation marks around it," my wife went on. "It is spelled *s–y–z–y–g–y.*" "You're kidding," I said, "there isn't any such word." Whereupon my wife reached for the dictionary. I returned to my reading with the smug assumption that she was wasting her time. Certainly nobody would spell a meaningful word in such an absurd fashion.

"You are wrong," said my wife triumphantly. "*Syzygy* does mean something. It's here in the dictionary. It comes from *syn,* meaning 'together,' and *zygon,* meaning 'yoke.' In astronomy, it means 'either of two opposing points in the orbit of a heavenly body, especially of the moon, at which it is in conjunction with or opposition to the sun.' "

I felt properly ignorant and retreated into silence quite certain nobody in his right mind would compose a word like *syzygy.* I am sure Noah Webster never heard of the word, and, if he had, he would have omitted it as an absurd conglomeration of letters of the alphabet.

My reading had been thoroughly disrupted by the mention of *syzygy,* and I got to thinking about words. It occurred to me that astronomers, biologists, chemists, and physicists use words that leave me feeling as if I were delving into a barrel of eels. My ignorance of some subjects is profound.

When I am in the area of my competence, I can read with intelligent understanding. The word *epistemology,* I know, concerns the theory of knowledge. *Ontology* is a branch of metaphysics dealing with the nature of being or reality. *Eschatology* deals with last things—death, resurrection, judgment, and immortality. I can find my way with a large assortment of words that might leave an engineer as puzzled as *syzygy* left me.

Syzygy was a tonic for my humility and made me acutely aware of my limitations. I felt somewhat like the distinguished schoolmaster who, one morning in class, was critical of a student who couldn't get his Latin conjugations straight. He was vigorously critical of the young man's incompetence. An hour later, the schoolmaster couldn't start his automobile. While he was struggling with the reluctant car, the student he had chastised stopped to ask if he could help. The young man raised the hood, tinkered with something, and remarked, "Now it should start." It did!

When we become aware of our own limitations, we are likely to be more patient with others. I may be at home in philosophy and theology and a neophyte in mechanics and may be comfortable in dealing with psychology and totally inept in physics. The more I think about the matter, the more I am aware that what I do not know would fill several large volumes.

It is something of a shock to our pride to discover the scope of our ignorance. Every time I have to call for a repairman to fix a refrigerator, dishwasher, or television, I am reminded that my knowledge of theology is no substitute for the knowledge of the repairman. He is distinctly superior to me when it comes to fixing balky gadgets.

Syzygy still bugs me. My wife won't let me forget my ignorance or my cocksureness in insisting there wasn't any such word. I hope that hereafter I'll remember how much I do not know.

Count the Silver Spoons

It may seem curious to those unfamiliar with the motivations behind human behavior, but our choices and decisions are guided by our beliefs and convictions. We often hear it said that actions are everything, while beliefs are unimportant. That, however, is colossal nonsense. The inescapable truth is that belief inspires behavior and leads to action, and action often depends on believing. We may well remind ourselves of what Dr. Johnson said to Boswell apropos of a man who denied the existence of a moral order. "If he does really think that there is no virtue and vice, why, sir, when he leaves the house, let us count the silver spoons." If men believe slaves are not fully human, they will treat them as animals.

John Milton, in *Paradise Lost*, records Satan's first speech, delivered to his lieutenant, Beelzebub. It is a grand defiance of God, a brilliant piece of rhetoric in which every phrase reveals his false set of values, his devastating hate, and his inordinate pride. Satan's third speech finds him a prisoner in hell and he proclaims himself its "new possessor." Then he suggests the nature of his perverted belief:

> To reign is worth ambition though in hell:
> Better to reign in hell than to serve in heaven.

Obviously, to believe it is "better to reign in hell than to serve in heaven" determined the behavior of Satan and his scorn of the values of truth and justice, love and mercy.

The other side of the coin, of course, is Milton's magnificent belief in God "whose service is perfect freedom." The hazard of our time lies not in the assumption that it is "better to reign in hell than to serve in heaven," but in the strange feeling that there are

163

no ultimate values to serve. Sadly enough, the belief that ultimate values no longer exist and the belief of Satan that to "reign in hell" is more to be desired than service in heaven lead to the same personal and social decay.

When psychologists speak of "conditioned responses," they mean responses to situations that become automatic. It should be noted, however, that our responses are conditioned by our beliefs. If God is dead and there are no ultimate values to serve, we are conditioned, like as not, to respond with expedience. A Chicago judge remarked concerning a prisoner on trial, "He has been conditioned to lie rather than to tell the truth." On the other hand, there are those like the late Gandhi, of whom it was said, "He is incapable of telling an untruth." We are blessed if we come to crises in our lives believing so deeply in truth and honor that we are incapable of deceit and dishonesty.

Abraham Lincoln, choosing to be honest rather than a United States senator, was coerced by his ultimate faith in integrity. He could do no other. The young man who stands up to moral strain in college or in the army does so because he is sustained by the flowing tide of his beliefs.

When Shakespeare's apothecary sold poison, suspecting it was intended for murder, he excused himself by saying, "My poverty, but not my will, consents." But his will did consent because he willed to be a party to murder rather than to continue in poverty. He had been conditioned to believe that security is more valuable than the will that ordains that we should live in honor.

Notice, if you will, that the choice of the apothecary to be a party to murder was but one facet of a life committed to its own security. So, in the absence of faith in God and belief that there are ultimate values to be served, an army had better be recruited to count the silver spoons.

Foundations for Tomorrow

... human kind
Cannot bear very much reality.
Time past and time future
What might have been and what has been
Point to one end, which is always present.

"Burnt Norton" by T. S. ELIOT

Not Stones, but Men

Marsilio Ficino, a friend of Lorenzo the Magnificent and one-time head of the Platonic Academy in Florence, insisted that "the city does not consist of stones, but of men; it is necessary to tend men like trees while they are young and guide them to bear fruit." Our cities still consist, not of stones, but of men and women on whose competence, integrity, and courage the future depends, men and women dedicated to the service of their fellowman.

Looking back across the centuries of our national life, it is clear that not only cities but also the nation have been fashioned by men and women who cared deeply for the common good. Like Abraham Lincoln and John Quincy Adams, Thomas Jefferson and James Madison, they were willing to sacrifice popularity for principle and idolatry of the crowd for ideals they cherished.

The creative leadership of dedicated men and women is costly. Their roles are lonely. In Boston, the rich, the cultivated, and the influential all turned against John Quincy Adams, whose principles seemed to undermine their interests. "I would not sit at the same table with that renegade," retorted one of Boston's leading citizens in refusing to attend a dinner at which Adams would be present.

One who aspires to honorable leadership is destined to be lonely. Over the life of a leader hangs an invisible inscription: all flattery abandon, ye who enter here. A good leader dares to speak the truth and to stand alone on principle. His mission often is distasteful and repugnant to special interests. He will not engage in semantic deception or hide behind rhetoric whose meaning is unclear. His speech is sincere and forthright.

167

No leader was more unjustly vilified than Lincoln. Through the dark days of the Civil War he was denounced and scorned as an incompetent. But in lonely grandeur, he stood against the storms. He was a great leader, not because he was clever, decisive in action, a good political showman, or an astute politician, but because his moral and spiritual leadership came first. As the words of his Gettysburg Address reveal, Lincoln was guided by the moral principle that a nation "conceived in liberty and dedicated to the proposition that all men are created equal" should not perish.

It is the unique quality of being able to see things whole in their moral and spiritual context that is distinctive of men and women on whom cities and nations are built. Situations beyond number are distorted by the influence of men and women who, as the Scriptures say, "see in part and prophesy in part." They see their own little, limited worlds. They live by their prejudices and in the darkness of their ignorance of larger issues that claim the minds of those who think with clarity.

There are politicians who "see in part," loyal to the pressure groups that helped to elect them. They are blind to the ultimate welfare of the nation. There are community leaders whose selfish interests lead them to "see in part" and to miss the vital concerns of the whole community.

Nations and cities, however, disintegrate and deteriorate, not because houses and buildings grow old, but because men and women "see in part" and care more for their own interests than for the good of the whole. Walter Lippmann put the issue clearly when he wrote, "We are challenged, every one of us, to think our way out of the terrors amidst which we live." Indeed, we are challenged to face the hard problems of our cities and our nation with intelligence and selfless courage if we are to emerge from the terrors of our time.

We need to cultivate a generation of men and women who will bear the heavy burdens of tomorrow with the fidelity, wisdom, and courage of those who founded the nation two hundred years ago. Somewhere there are men like Madison and Jefferson, John Quincy Adams and George Washington lurking in our society, unassuming men of competence and insight, able to take up the challenge of leadership.

The portrait of Washington at Valley Forge, written by Viney
Wilder Endicott, suggests the character of the men and women
the nation needs:

> I like to vision him beneath the stars
> On those grim winter nights when faith was low.
> I like remembering he kneeled in prayer
> At Valley Forge, surrounded by the foe.
>
> I like remembering his quiet strength
> When chaos clambered at his side;
> He worked and planned and left the rest to God
> And gained new wisdom that would turn the tide.

Mediocrity Isn't Enough

The evolution of our industrial society has resulted in undermining the significance of individuals. Alexis de Tocqueville long ago detected a dislike of great men in democratic society. Democracy, he noted, has a tendency to encourage mediocrity. As we live and work more and more in large organizations, both the bureaucrat and "the organization man" have become symbols of the system.

We need to be reminded of Plato's comment that "what is honored in a country will be cultivated there." If we honor mediocrity, it will be cultivated in our society. If "the organization man" getting along by going along is honored, we will cultivate men and women lacking independent integrity and initiative. We will come in the end to what Dr. Zhivago called "the spiritual ceiling of the age."

Studies of inner-city schools suggest that those who achieve beyond their fellows are punished by their peers. It is not acceptable for a student to rise above his contemporaries, and it takes great courage and motivation for him to make the most of himself. Even in the affluent suburbs, peer groups tend to level academic achievement. One youngster explained his poor record in high school by saying, "I just don't want the gang to think I'm a brain."

It should be noted, however, that, in a free society, the best men and women make the best citizens. Totalitarian societies fear their best people and often resort to liquidating those of independent mind. The observation of John Stuart Mill, however, is worth noting. He warned that a state that reduces men and women to docile instruments, even for beneficial purposes, will find that little men accomplish nothing great.

If our society honors mediocrity and nourishes men and women

170

who are satisfied to be other-directed, docile instruments of the organization, it will create nothing essentially great. Mill said that "the greatness of England is now all collective." He added, "Individually small, we only appear capable of anything great by our habit of combining." He could have been writing for us at a time when we seem to believe in the superiority of the team and the committee. Mill concluded soberingly, "It was men of another stamp than this that made England what it has been; and men of another stamp will be needed to prevent its decline."

The problem of our time is underproductive people, unwilling to stretch their minds with hard thinking; unwilling to give the little more that is so much to their labors; unwilling to expand their powers by assuming new responsibilities; unwilling to risk independence for the sake of their integrity. What we need are men and women of another stamp.

Somewhere I read the comment that "the reefs of history are strewn with the wreckage of republics." Republics have foundered, not because their ideals were unsound, but because people grew weary of responsibility and struggle. They yielded to the persuasions of mediocrity and sacrificed the spirit of initiative and independence, having reached "the spiritual ceiling of the age."

There is enough vitality in our society to alter the current of our nation and renew the creative spirit of its people. Although initiative and independence have been muted, they are not dead. As Charles A. Beard, the historian, wrote, "Calamities may come upon America," but "enough of our republic will be kept intact to restore, rebuild, and go ahead. Surely, Americans will endlessly strive to carry on the values in their heritage."

John Keats' prayer for England is appropriate for us:

> In the long vistas of the years to roll,
> Let me not see our country's honor fade;
> O let me see our land regain her soul,
> Her pride, her freedom.

The Capacity to Inflict Pain

When a Harvard University president was asked to name the fundamental quality essential to leadership, he replied, "The capacity to inflict pain." That is a blunt way of saying that leadership requires courage to speak the unvarnished truth, however unpopular it may be, to face reality without blinking, and to make hard choices that are painful but necessary.

Winston Churchill revealed that quality of leadership. He galvanized the energies of the British people during World War II, promising only "blood, sweat, toil, and tears." He asked people to accept heroic suffering and to rise above their agony until they achieved their "finest hour." And the British accepted the challenge with courage and dignity.

It is unfortunate that today England's leadership lacks "the capacity to inflict pain." The necessary, hard decisions are being postponed in the vain hope that the nation can "muddle through" its current problems without sacrifice, without "blood, sweat, toil, and tears."

In similar fashion, political leaders in our own land seem to lack this indispensable quality. Neither Republicans nor Democrats appear able to make necessary decisions that will inflict pain. Both parties want painless solutions to our social ills. As a consequence, Will Rogers noted, "There is something about a Republican that you can only stand him just so long; and there is something about a Democrat that you can't stand him quite that long."

Neither Democrats nor Republicans are willing to deal rigorously with the welfare mess, even though welfare dependency has increased more than threefold in the last ten years. It is easier for politicians to ignore the problem than to risk the political hazards of making needed changes. It is simpler and safer to leave things alone than to face the issue with honest realism.

Because our leaders are unwilling to inflict pain, the energy crisis worsens. More than thirty years ago, I listened to an oil executive pleading for action to avoid just such a crisis. Nobody would listen to him or take him seriously. The political leaders to whom he spoke and wrote shrugged off his arguments because they were unwilling to inflict pain on their constituents. The mental climate of political Washington reflected what once was said about a senator—that for him "even a mushroom cloud had a silver lining."

We as a people need to be called to account, to face the self-discipline and sacrifice we need to emerge from the ills of the present. "We will have to learn to walk more and ride less," a thoughtful man remarked. "There never will be an end of the need for exertion, hard work, and intellectual effort. We have had it too easy for too long."

If some political leader would speak to us with candor and honesty, I dare say he would gather a significant following. If he would challenge us to sacrifice, sweat, and even tears, I think we might respond. If he would dare to propose tough programs designed to keep the nation solvent and deal with the energy crisis and the welfare mess, I am persuaded the nation would be grateful for his stringency.

As a people, we have within us the moral gumption to do what we must to meet the problems we face. We are politically mature enough to accept hard facts clearly presented and make necessary and painful choices. We are wise enough to know that the strength of the nation lies in our courage, faith, initiative, and toil. But the nation requires leaders, men and women of integrity and dedication to the common good, who are thoughtful and willing to speak the hard truth and ready, when required, to inflict pain.

Reasoning Together

In a free society, opposition on the part of others is not only legally permissible; it is spiritually indispensable. We advance by way of contraries, sharpening our minds on creative controversy. The wise executive surrounds himself with men who are capable of independent judgment, not with "yes men." The government leader clarifies his own thinking in the vigorous give and take of debate.

There is a passage in Isaiah that reads in the Revised Standard Version of the Bible, "Come, let us reason together." In the New English Bible, the passage reads, "Come, let us argue it out." The former translation suggests a quiet thinking together, seeking answers to difficult problems; the latter translation suggests the hard slugging of debate.

It should be observed that there is a place for both the quiet reasoning together and for the slugging debate. The clue to creativity, however, is the capacity in both cases to seek what truth there may be in an opponent's point of view.

There is a hint of wisdom in the argument suggested by a book reviewer who wrote, "A good critic is not someone who is always right but someone who always convinces us that the work he is criticizing deserves our attention." When we face opposition, we need to recognize that the points of view from which we differ still deserve careful attention. We keep our cool because we wish to discover what may be worthy of examination in the arguments of the opposition.

Commonly, we make the mistake of writing off the opposition as either ignorant or prejudiced. As Ko-Ko sang in The Mikado, there are people "who wouldn't be missed." However, as Robert Frost wrote perceptively in "The Census Taker":

> If one by one we counted people out
> For the least fault, it wouldn't take us long
> To get so we had no one left to live with.

So, if we write off those who do not agree with us, count them out, it won't be long before we have "no one left to live with."

Nobody is right all the time, and perspectives make a vast difference in the way we see problems and issues. We will understand our differences with greater clarity if we keep cool enough to perceive the varying perspectives from which we view problems. Our views are as different as our major concerns, as is suggested in the comments of a parson, a geologist, and a cowboy on seeing the Grand Canyon for the first time: "One of the wonders of God," said the parson; "one of the wonders of science," said the geologist; "what a hell of a place to raise a cow," said the cowboy.

One of the tragedies of our time is rigidity, and often the young are as rigid as the old. The young take positions on varying issues in somewhat the spirit of William Ewart Gladstone, of whom it was said that "his tendency was to believe his desires were those of the Almighty. He was reproached, not so much for always having the ace of trumps up his sleeve as for claiming that God had put it there." It is impossible to reason together, or even to argue it out, when one party to the discussion is sure his desires are those of the Almighty.

On the other hand, the old frequently do not listen. At a meeting of the American Society of Newspaper Editors, former Governor Ronald Reagan was asked if he ever had wished to have direct contact with young demonstrators. He answered that often he would go out with them and say, "Listen. . . ."

The communication barrier is suggested by Reagan's remark. We want other people to do the listening. The young want the old to listen, and the old want the young to listen. Unfortunately, nobody seems to be hearing what others have to say. It is time for us to listen and to reason together.

Apathy and Aspiration

Most of us who have passed the midstream of life have lived through one crisis after another: wars and rumors of wars, depression and high taxes, cold war, industrial conflict, race struggle, and world revolution. It may be that our aspirations and our faith have been undermined by prolonged stress and tension. We have heard the cry "Wolf, wolf" so often that we no longer listen.

Psychologists tell us that long periods of tension often lead to apathy. At least for the moment, that is where we seem to be. Richard L. Strout, writing from Washington, says there is a ho-hum mood in the capital, and Richard Rovere, a magazine writer, notes "the immense political presence of public apathy. It deadens the air and muffles and muddles controversy." We rather wish the disturbers would leave us alone and not bother us about unemployment, the energy crisis, problems of race, or nuclear danger.

Our apathy is partly the consequence of our feeling of futility. We suspect that the bigness of things has made us into political, economic, and social ciphers. We have come to the conclusion that we really can't do anything to relieve the tensions of our time or create a better world. Margaret Mead portrayed our mood when she wrote, "We've grown oppressed by a sense that the world's gotten so big and unmanageable that it is very hard for individuals to be able to influence it very much."

If we can't control the world, we may as well retreat to our gardens and television sets. As Calvin Kytle wrote, "Whereas not too long ago we were moved to find ourselves in a group, nowadays we seem to want to lose ourselves in a crowd."

We appear to have forgotten that, in the economy of God, each of us counts for one. The more of us there are who retreat, the fewer of us there are to deal with the bigness of the world. We can assume "The City of God" won't be built and deny responsibility, but the more of us there are who default, the fewer there will be to act creatively. We are not ciphers unless we wish to join the crowd in retreat.

In a free society, we are involved in a collective effort to create the good society, but every individual is responsible for his own portion of the social fabric. A youngster in prep school wrote to his father explaining a football defeat with simple honesty. "The opposition came through a big hole in our line," he wrote. Then he added, "The hole was me."

The words suggest a hard truth about the nature of society. When the absence of justice or righteousness or courage in contemporary life leads to setbacks for a free society, many of us can say, if we are honest, "the hole was me."

Some years ago, a minister in Georgia, sensing the rising tide of racial tension, undertook to get acquainted with leaders in the black community. He did the unforgivable. He invited them to his home and made them aware that he understood their feelings and would do what he could to create a better climate of understanding between blacks and whites. He worked at it incessantly until he retired, leaving a legacy that would not be soon forgotten. One man plugged the hole where he was.

What we need today are men and women of intellectual and spiritual spine who will articulate the ethics of mature people, who will undertake to plug the holes where they are. Tensions in society should be creative, not destructive, and can be if we dare to meet them with courage and with reason undergirded by faith.

Courage at Midnight

When Winston Churchill made a catalog of human virtues, he put courage at the top of the list. Although some of us would put love at the apex of a pyramid of virtues, there is no doubt that courage should rank high. The dictionary defines *courage* as "the attitude or response of facing and dealing with anything recognized as dangerous, difficult, or painful instead of withdrawing from it."

Most of us confront the difficult or painful, if not the dangerous, with consistent regularity. Should we go on with the rat race, struggling against odds in the business world, or throw in the towel? Should we keep faith through periods of difficulty in marriage, or chuck it and try again? Should we go on in a tough job, full of discouragement and frustration, or quit? When grades are poor and teachers seem unsympathetic, should students withdraw or go on with the battle?

There is nothing particularly dramatic about the commonplace choices we have to make in the face of difficulty, but it takes high courage to decide with dignity. It may be easier for a soldier to stand by his post at the cost of his life than for a failing student to take himself in hand and come through. It may require more fortitude for a man to cope with his business anxieties than for a sea captain to stand by his sinking ship.

Midnights come to us all, when we wonder if it is worth our while to go on in the face of discouragement and even defeat. Nevertheless, the courage with which a man or woman deals with the worst is the measure of the person. Who can calculate the courage of a young woman crippled by the ravages of polio but carrying on cheerfully despite her limitations or the stature of a man going on with gentleness and grace after his young wife died, leaving three small children?

Inevitably, we are confronted by anxiety when our midnights come, leaving us hurt and bewildered. Nevertheless, as Washington Gladden wrote in "Ultima Veritas":

> In the darkest night of the year,
> When the stars have all gone out

those who are wise are sure

> That courage is better than fear,
> That faith is truer than doubt.

The world is made better by men and women whose courage is sustained by their faith, so that they are able to push on with cheerful strength.

Paul Tillich, one of the great philosophical theologians of our time, wrote of the "courage to be," which has three characteristics, the first of which is courage to be part of a larger whole, to be involved in human relationships. Involvement inevitably means the acceptance of risk. It takes courage to love because love involves the risk of being hurt or disappointed. What is more, to love is to suffer with those we love, to feel their failures, their mistakes, their pain. To love is to feel the anguish of the poor and the dispossessed and to seek remedies for their plight. Only the courageous dare to love.

There is, then, a second characteristic of the "courage to be," namely, the courage to be one's self and to stand alone as an independent person. It is refusal to be pushed by the tide of opinion, willingness to swim against the current in obedience to the best we know. It is determination to stand by values that are lasting and eternal despite the pressures of society.

The third characteristic of the "courage to be" is the courage to be sustained by the creative power of God, "the ground of our being." It is to find undergirding spiritual strength to be involved, to love, and to stand with courage in the face of difficulty, pain, or danger. It is to know that, in our strivings for the decent and the good, we are sustained by a Power beyond ourselves that is forever working for the loving, the good, and the true.

In the commonplace courage of every day, the issues of personal life and society are decided.

Train Whistle at Church

Looking back over the years to her childhood, a perceptive woman recalled driving in a surrey from her farm home to church in a small town. Sitting in a church pew with her family, there were times when her mind wandered from the sermon. She remembered that, at 11:15 A.M., a passenger train was due to whistle for a crossing, and she would listen for the sound with anticipation.

"The train whistle," the lady recalled, "seemed to be saying, 'Something is waiting out there in the world. Go and find it.'" There was more beyond the little village, the one-room school, the country store, and the farm. These, to be sure, would form a solid base for adventuring beyond, but the call to reach out was implicit in the sound of the train whistle while she sat in the church.

The child's dreams of the world beyond have been realized in the years since the train whistle charmed her imagination. She has traveled throughout the world and caught the flavor of many cultures, making friends in many lands and leaving life better than she found it wherever she traveled.

Ralph Waldo Emerson understood the call of the beyond and the meaning of a life reaching out to others. Concord, Massachusetts, was his base, but he traveled to the Continent and to Great Britain, where he visited Thomas Carlyle, whose works he had read with appreciation. Carlyle's fortunes were at a low ebb when, as he said, Emerson came "like an angel in the night." Later, he wrote to his Concord friend to say that "in joy or grief a voice says to me, 'Behold there is one that loves thee; in thy loneliness, in thy darkness, see how a hospitable candle shines from afar over seas, how a friendly heart watches!' It is very good, and precious to me." Emerson was indeed a friend to Carlyle.

Wherever Emerson traveled, he carried with him characteristics of mind and spirit nurtured in Concord, where his roots went deep. And no matter how far distant the train whistle called a child in church, as an adult she was aware her mind and spirit had been fashioned in the little village she remembers with gratitude. Her yearning to know and to understand the world and its people was inspired in the little one-room school, with its potbellied stove and desks carved with the initials of students from the past.

We always make our best excursions into the unknown from a base we can trust, from a place where ideals are cherished and values are sound. We push out into the world at large with vision, confidence, and hope from homes and churches that have nourished the best in ourselves and made us aware of our own possibilities and potential for greatness.

It is significant, I think, that a train whistle captured the imagination of a child while she sat in church. The church offered a solid and dependable anchor for her venturing out into the world, with its challenges and disappointments, its hardships and hurts. If the sermons she heard were trite at times and the music left something to be desired, still she was made aware that there is "an anchor, sure and steadfast" for life.

We take into the world something of the flavor of our childhood experience. If childhood is warped by cruelty or the absence of love, adulthood is likely to be selfish and narrow. If childhood is devoid of ideals and moral standards, the later years will bear the marks of the past. Visions of a world to be conquered are muted if the base from which we move is as shifting sand.

What of the children of today and tomorrow? Will they dream? Of course they will dream, as children always do, of the wide world beyond where they are. Train whistles have been replaced by the roar of jet planes, but the young will hear the call of the beyond, of something waiting to be found. Will they have dependable bases from which to make their ventures into the unknown? Will they find ideals and values they can trust in the homes they share? Will they hear the call of the beyond in churches that point to things that are precious for life?

The future hinges on the soundness of the bases from which our children venture.

Education for What?

The Renaissance was a period of intellectual, artistic, and spiritual awakening. Erasmus showered the benefits of his great learning on his contemporaries. Michelangelo, Botticelli, Raphael, and Leonardo da Vinci created things of beauty to be "a joy forever." Humanism was the fad of the day, and there were renewed efforts both to understand the past and to prepare for the future.

In contemporary thought, a high measure of praise is heaped on one of whom it can be said he is "a man of the Renaissance." The Renaissance man may be described as one of well-rounded ability, whose view of the world is comprehensive and whose knowledge is not only useful but also a source of personal and social enrichment. The Renaissance man is one whose learning has been translated into wisdom.

Modern education would do well to dedicate itself to developing well-rounded students whose knowledge is infused with wisdom and insight. The trend toward specialization, with an emphasis on science, which has been characteristic of education through the past quarter of a century, has provided students with greater factual knowledge but scanty spiritual and ethical information for other than a naturalistic view of life. Students have been learning "more about less and less about more" until life for many has lost its sense of meaning.

Nathan M. Pusey, in *The Age of the Scholar*, enunciated the need for both the Renaissance man and woman when he wrote, "Our job is to educate free, independent, and vigorous minds capable of analyzing events, of exercising judgment, or distinguishing between facts and propaganda and truth from half-truths and lies, and in the most creative among them at least—of apprehending further reaches of truth. It is also our responsibility

182

to see that these minds are embedded in total persons who will stand with faith and courage, and always, too, in thoughtful concern for others."

So, education is not primarily a matter of creating replicas of Oliver Goldsmith's village schoolmaster, whose contemporaries gazed upon him

> ... and still the wonder grew,
> That one small head could carry all he knew.

Fact-filled marvels, crammed full of factual knowledge, may be neither good nor wise, creative nor productive. Knowledge is a primary tool for the ability to think both creatively and ethically.

"We must educate! We must educate! or we must perish by our own prosperity," Lyman Beecher wrote in 1835. He understood that without education for complete living our "haste to be rich and mighty" would outrun both our wisdom and our ethical concern. We would, he thought, be pushed into bondage to material wealth and destroyed by our spiritual ennui.

We cannot guess what the needs of the next century will be, except that it will require men and women of imagination, courage, wisdom, and compassion. Stereotypes of thought will leave us helpless before the relentless march of time and change, but a capacity for creative thought will enable today's students to solve the problems of the future as they come upon them.

Mark Hopkins had no wish to cram the heads of his students with facts, even though he had a high respect for facts. He wanted his students to know what they needed to know and as much as they could know, but, as his biographer noted, "He sought to train them to think their way into the heart of things, and to think in such fashion that life would have meaning and that they could use their powers to the best advantage." It is in "thinking their way into the heart of things" that contemporary students will be able to meet the problems of the future.

It may be that our time of stress will lead us to educate Renaissance men and women, who are able to think, analyze events, exercise judgment, recognize abiding values, and "stand with faith and courage" in "thoughtful concern for others." If we do, there will be young men and women able to assume roles of leadership in our tomorrows. They will be persons of high character and purpose, adequate for the demands of the future.

Our Town

A young man, just beginning his life in the ministry, was called to a little town in eastern Kansas in the dust-bowl days of 1932. Both dust and depression had settled over the town, and the church, run down at the heels and needing paint, was on its last legs. The young preacher wrote back to his seminary alma mater, "This place sure is an ugly duckling, but it needs somebody to love it."

Needless to say, the little church that found somebody to love it began to thrive, and it turned out to be anything but an ugly duckling. In the same fashion, when a home, a business, a city, or an idea finds somebody to love it, it takes on new vitality and dynamic. But things get run down at the heels in a hurry if nobody cares.

Possibly your town has turned into an ugly duckling, with crime or corruption, or both, eating at its heart. It can happen in no time at all when nobody really loves the place enough to do something about it. It is happening all over this beloved land of ours, and the sad part is that we don't seem to care too much. Maybe we are just too preoccupied with our own affairs to look beyond our own plodding feet. At any rate, too many of our cities are turning into ugly ducklings.

Now and then, somebody who really loves his town rolls up his sleeves and resolves to do something. He is grateful for the place that gave him his chance in life, for all the memories that cluster around the town in which he was born. He can't quite forget the old school, where, despite his perverse resistance to learning, he absorbed enough to make him aware of his heritage. Somehow it hurts to have the town spoiled by people who want to use it just to feather their own nests. He would like to keep the place the way it ought to be for the generations yet to come. So he goes to work with a will, only to be discouraged by people who don't care.

Once, in a town that I loved, a corrupt political machine was making the place an ugly duckling. I decided to do something, but it was a disillusioning experience. Everybody agreed somebody ought to do something, but everybody had good reasons for doing nothing. Most of the people were like the man fishing beside a drawbridge that had been raised, but the safety gates had failed to close. The fisherman watched a blind man fumbling his way toward the bridge. "Somebody ought to stop him or he'll fall in," he said to himself, and then he went on with his fishing. There was a yell and a splash, and the fisherman said to himself, "Well, he's fallen in. I knew it would happen."

Where are the people who care if the town falls into the ditch? Mostly, I suspect, they feel like Moses standing before the burning bush, asking himself, "Who am I that I should lead this people?" The Bible says that Moses was "slow of speech"—maybe he stuttered, for all I know. Getting his people out of Egypt looked like a rugged assignment. It seemed as impossible as getting a town out of the hands of a political machine. But it wasn't impossible. The Promised Land was not an idle dream.

In his stirring play, *The Firstborn*, Christopher Fry puts the problem plainly on the lips of Moses:

> I need to know how good
> Can be strong enough to break out of the possessing
> Arms of evil.

Then, he adds reflectively:

> Somewhere, not beyond our scope, is a power
> Participating but unharnessed, waiting
> To be led toward us. Good has a singular strength
> Not known to evil.

When we face the problems of our town, do we dare to believe that "good has a singular strength not known to evil"? Will we risk our lives and our reputations on the conviction that "good can be strong enough to break out of the possessing arms of evil"?

These are vital questions as we face the future of our town. And the answers lie in our own will and determination.

We are just ordinary, run-of-the-mill men and women, you and I, but we are not as helpless as we think, and when we begin to love our town enough to do something, our town will stop being an ugly duckling. The good we stand for and believe in has "a singular strength" when we let it use our hands and minds. Our towns need a lot of somebodies to love them.

Inward Retreat

There is a trend in modern thought and therapy that seeks to deify the isolated self. As Peter Marin has suggested, "Selfishness and moral blindness now assert themselves . . . as enlightenment and psychic health." Self-realization and self-fulfillment are the watchwords of contemporary society.

In the new psychological economy, the self replaces God as the arbiter of value: whatever enhances the self is good, and whatever imposes burdens on the self is bad. One young couple articulated the current mood by saying, "Without children we can have a ball. We don't want the burden and inconvenience of children." In the economy of the private self, there is no room for concern for the collective good.

There is an inner restlessness in all of us, a yearning for fulfillment in our lives. We are disposed to think naively that our ethical inhibitions thwart the possibilities of self-satisfaction. And we conclude that, if we could learn to defend ourselves against the demands of conscience by deifying ourselves, life would be a song. Seeking only private self-realization, we can avoid the demands of the world and smother the summons of conscience.

In many ways, the new therapies of self-realization are a revival of the ancient philosophy of hedonism, which holds that pleasure is the principal good and should be the aim of all action. The private self is the arbiter of behavior, and the only evil is that which thwarts the pleasure of the self. Unfortunately, the doctrine obscures all ethical responsibility and all sense of community.

"I've tried everything," a young man said, "pot, sex, Zen, transcendental meditation—you name it. But the fact is—I hate myself." He had set out to find himself, to fulfill himself, as he put

187

it, but his adventure with self-deification left him with his last state worse than his first.

Robert Browning remarked perceptively that "man seeks only his own good at the whole world's cost." He might have added that man seeks only his own good at his own cost, too. The life committed only to the demands of the self tends to lead to self-hatred, not to self-fulfillment. The quest for private self-realization that excludes other-concern and ethical values results not in happiness, but in misery.

There is a vastly larger world than the self—a world of human relationships, of community, of spiritual and moral values. It is the larger world that impinges upon us and from which we cannot escape. Its ghostly presence invades the sanctuary of the private self and refuses to depart. The economy of God overwhelms the economy of the self.

John Steinbeck came to terms with the issue in the difficult days before he achieved success as a writer. In a letter to his friend and literary agent, Elizabeth Otis, Steinbeck wrote, "Make no compromise at all for financial considerations . . . we've gone through too damned much trying to keep the work honest and in a state of improvement to let it slip now in consideration of a little miserable popularity."

No doubt "a little miserable popularity" and money would have yielded a degree of pleasure, but Steinbeck recognized the ultimate significance of the larger world of ethical and spiritual values. He was aware of the unique importance of his integrity as a writer and his honesty with his readers. He could not fulfill himself apart from the larger world that embraced others, including God, as well as himself. Steinbeck voiced the essence of the matter when he noted that, as a writer, "I can create something that is larger and richer than I am."

It is concern for the "something that is larger and richer than I am" that enables us to escape from our inward prisons and find the deepest and most abiding satisfactions life affords. The deified self is the imprisoned, self-hating self.

Persistent Prejudices

Our prejudices are persistent. They invade our thinking and push us to irrational conclusions. In subtle and often unconscious ways, they corrupt reason with feeling and distort our responses to human problems. H. G. Wells noted the phenomenon when he wrote that "the power of most of the great prejudices that strain humanity lies deeper than the intellectual level."

A *prejudice,* says the dictionary, is a "preconceived judgment or opinion leaning toward one side of a question from other considerations than those belonging to it." No one of us entirely escapes the hazard of undigested emotional experience that shunts us off the main line of issues onto some spur line that leads to conflict. We have touchy spots, feel intense likes or dislikes that, on rational grounds, are unaccountable.

The difficulty with a prejudice is that it resists logical discussion and argument. Emotions are not arguable. They sit on our minds with the authority of a decided opinion that resists all attempts to dislodge it. We find it incredibly difficult, for example, to talk rationally about integration in our schools or bussing to accomplish integration because our minds are clouded by our prejudices.

One unfortunate experience reported by someone else or endured by ourselves easily translates itself into a universal that clouds our perception of reality. Confrontations between black and white, between parents and children, between labor and management have emotional overtones that thwart both understanding and conciliation. Each side confronts the other with preconceived opinions leaning toward one or the other side of a question, and neither side will listen to the other.

189

The mental and emotional habits that compose our prejudices are often the consequence of what R. T. Halsam called "label thinking." It is suggested by such commonly heard expressions as "business versus government," "labor versus management," "common man versus the establishment," "black versus white." Such phrases suggest that the relationship between groups is one of conflict and that their objectives are different.

If we are aware that our overreactions against unions or blacks, government or the establishment point to some old vulnerability in ourselves, some upsetting experience, or some thwarted self-interest, we may be able to approach conflict with deeper insight and clearer understanding of the issues. At the very least, we need to look into ourselves to discover the sources of our feeling and prejudices.

The spirit of tolerance, born of deeper self-understanding, does not necessarily negate the way we feel. It makes us aware, however, that our responses involve more than logic. We can never be really tolerant in the sense of pretending that everyone can think as he desires and that one conviction is as good as another. We still make our claims. We shall make them, however, in the light of our fundamental convictions as to where reality lies, seeking honestly to see the issues apart from feelings we have recognized as irrational.

Above all, I suspect, we need to be patient with ourselves and with others. Some years ago, a distinguished black professor wrote a rather dark, and in places bitter, book about his own race. In the course of the book he wrote: "I believe in patience—patience with the weakness of the weak and the strength of the strong; the prejudice of the ignorant and the ignorance of the blind; patience with the tardy triumph of joy and the mad chastening of sorrow—patience with God."

When we look into ourselves with honest eyes to ferret out our prejudices and to separate our feelings from our reason, we may very well discover that we have distorted reality and perverted truth, not intentionally, perhaps, but unconsciously. We may then be prepared to be patient with ourselves, patient, but ready to reconsider, and patient with the prejudices of others.

Failure While Daring Greatness

The poet Ovid cherished the notion of "failure while daring greatness." Like Oscar Wilde, he understood that it is one thing to have "success without dignity, and failure without pathos," but it is something else to dare great things with dignity and to fail with courage and undiminished self-respect.

It is quite possible to succeed without self-respect—to win the world and lose one's soul. Revelations of business success through bribery and political power won by corruption suggest a commonplace unwillingness to risk "failure while daring greatness." The assumption seems to be that it is better to succeed without dignity and to achieve without self-respect than to risk failure with honor.

Greatness requires a quality of moral grandeur that rejects the little aims that end with self in favor of loyalty to the royal in one's self. The successful rogue is a failure. Triumph without ethical dignity is an illusion. Wealth won in dishonor is tasteless. There is no daring or greatness in life that is unwilling to risk failure for the sake of the values that give meaning to life.

The emptiness of life devoid of ethical integrity and spiritual commitment is suggested in H. G. Wells' description of the Young Man about Town in "The Research Magnificent": "He saw it all as a joyless indulgence, as a confusion of playthings and undisciplined desires, as a succession of days that began amiably and weakly, that became steadily more crowded and ignoble and the trivial occupations, that had sunken now to indignity and uncleanness."

Somehow the futility of life without integrity and worthy commitments got to the Young Man about Town, and suddenly he reached out his arms in the darkness and prayed aloud to the silences, "O God, give me back my visions." The cry is a haunting

191

one that finds echoes in those who find life meaningless and empty, wishing that they could recover their visions and their self-respect.

In a success-oriented world, no one wants to fail. If the price of success is cutting moral corners, we comfort ourselves with the idea that "everybody is doing it." Too many people are doing it to their own cost and to the detriment of our free society. "Democracy," as Justice Louis D. Brandeis noted in 1923, "substitutes self-restraint for external restraint. It demands continuous sacrifice by the individual and more exigent obedience to the moral law than any other form of government."

There is scarcely any heresy more damaging than the notion that we can live happily and well simply by "doin' what comes naturally." G. K. Chesterton put the point with characteristic terseness when he wrote, "In everything on this earth that is worth doing, there is a stage when no one would do it except for necessity or honor." There are "oughts" that get in the way of what comes naturally, and they challenge us to dare greatness, even at the risk of failure.

Our own lives and the society we share depend for their well-being on men and women who are obedient to the "oughts" they recognize as the claims of God. John Marshall, the great chief justice of the United States Supreme Court in the formative years of the nation, attributed ethical ideals to the Creator. A few years after him, Justice Joseph Storey maintained that all high principles of society are eternal obligations arising from our common dependence on God.

There is a striking passage in Paul's letter to the Romans wherein the great apostle noted that "the wrath of God is revealed ...against...men who by their own wickedness suppress the truth." When men complained they did not know right from wrong, Paul made it clear they were "without excuse." They did know, but "claiming to be wise, they become fools."

We know we ought to dare the greatness of moral grandeur, but too often we are unwilling to risk the possibility of failure on the altar of integrity and truth. We know what we ought to say and do, but we would rather not do it. We rationalize our wants and wishes and make the worse appear the better part, but "claiming to be wise," we "become fools." Nevertheless, despite ourselves, we are called to greatness.

192